CH00792602

Switchword Miracles

Creating Miracles, One Word At A Time

Doron Alon

Switchword Miracles.

Copyright © 2012 by Doron Alon
Published and distributed by: Numinosity Press Incorporated.

All rights reserved. No part of this book may be reproduced by
any mechanical, photographic, or electrical process, or in the form
of a recording. Nor may it be stored in a storage/retrieval system
nor transmitted or otherwise be copied for private or public use-
other than "fair use" as quotations in articles or reviews—without
the prior written consent of the Author and Numinosity Press
Incorporated.

The Information in this book is solely for educational purposes
and not for the treatment, diagnosis or prescription of any
diseases. This text is not meant to provide financial or health
advice of any sort. The Author and the publisher are in no way
liable for any use or misuse of the material.

Alon, Doron .
Switchword Miracles –1st ed
ISBN: 978-0-9824722-1-7
Printed in the United States of America
Book Cover Design: Created by Shahnaz Mohammed
NAZNYC@GMAIL.COM
Cover image: Yoga & Spirituality. © *LUCELUCELUCE -
FOTOLIA.COM*
Image on Pg 66 © M.Gove - Fotolia.com

DEDICATION

Dedicated to You

TABLE OF CONTENTS

Dedication

Table of Contents

Introduction

Chapter 1: The Subconscious Mind

Chapter 2: Chronic Symptoms Of Self Sabotage

Chapter 3: The Chain Reaction

Chapter 4: The Energy System / Getting Clear

Chapter 5: Meridian Tapping

Chapter 6: Switchwords

Chapter 7: Putting The Pieces Together

Conclusion

Contact Information

INTRODUCTION

I want to take this time to thank you for sharing your time with me by purchasing this book. From the millions of books out there on self-improvement and spirituality, I am honored and grateful you chose this one. What you are about to read can CHANGE your life, often within days and maybe even sooner. I wrote this book specifically for people like you who want and need to make radical changes now. I know many books and courses say they teach quick ways to achieve shifts in consciousness, but this is different.

What makes this book different is that the two modalities covered are very powerful; when they are combined, they can produce powerful shifts in your consciousness. This shift in consciousness is what you need to start making changes in the areas of your life you most need help with. Unlike other modalities that require you to have faith that they will work, these modalities work regardless of whether you believe in them or not. The combination consists of Meridian Tapping (more popularly known as E.F.T) and Switchwords. Switchwords are a little-known modality that changes lives. It works like magic, and yet; it is not very well-known. Alone, both modalities are powerful tools of transformation. Together, they are unstoppable.

I have studied and experimented with many spiritual modalities over the past 23 years and have encountered some wonderful tools. My endless curiosity for all things spiritual and my drive to create practical and powerful tools of transformation have led me to this point. My goal in writing this book was to present these powerful concepts in a language and in a manner that will make it accessible to everyone. I am of the belief that change doesn't have to cost someone thousands of dollars to learn and achieve.

If you use the methods contained in this book with an open mind and heart, you will see results immediately. I know that is a bold statement to make, but this is based not only on my own experiences with both Meridian Tapping and Switchwords, but also of thousands of people who have used the individual methods contained in this book. The reason these two modalities work so well together is because they both bypass the subconscious mind's resistance. They work on the subconscious mind in slightly different ways yet are complementary and have a wonderful synergistic effect.

When combining Meridian Tapping and Switchwords you are going to start stirring the subconscious mind. Usually the Subconscious mind doesn't like to relinquish old patterns without a fight; it LOVES repetition and habit and will not easily give these comforts up.

The beauty of combining these two modalities is that there will be very little fighting from the subconscious mind, and if there is; it will be brief. I know that is hard to believe, I didn't believe it at first until I tried it out for myself. Within a few days, I was a new person. I am not exaggerating. I finally started to gain control over my subconscious mind in such a way that I could reverse old destructive patterns that were ruining my life. It's important to get control because if patterns persist, they will run your life into the ground. Carl Jung said it best when he said, "You must make the unconscious, conscious, otherwise it will control your life, and you will call it fate." This is a powerful statement.

Let me ask you…

Have you ever acted in ways that embarrassed you or others?
Have you acted in ways that shocked you?
Do you have a repetitive behavior or addiction you know is bad for you, but yet you can't stop it?
Do you have recurrent nightmares?
Do you find yourself spending money recklessly despite already having a ton of debt?
Do you often feel out of control?
Do you have a hard time achieving your goals and objectives?

Most likely, the answer to one or more of these questions is yes. I can relate. I have answered yes to every one of those questions. I have self-sabotaged countless times and in so many ways and over many years. One day, however, I hit a wall …I just had it; I was crying every day, not just crying, but seriously balling until I felt like passing out. I was drinking myself into oblivion every day and isolating myself from the world and the worst part of it for me was that I lost a woman I truly-loved because of my behavior. I gained a good 20 lbs as well. It was a dark time and in all honesty, I relished the idea of death. I would have fantasies about killing myself, and that idea would give me solace. Can you believe that? Yes, it was that bad.

I had to gain control, if I didn't, you wouldn't be reading these words. As Jung implies, these behaviors and habits that seem out of your control are, in fact, very much within your control, you just need a little help like I did. The only way to expose these behaviors and habits of thinking is to defuse them in a way that won't cause a sudden backlash from the subconscious mind. Self-Sabotaging behaviors are the subconscious minds attempt at expressing, but also protecting you from repressed and unaddressed issues in your life. It also serves as a playback mechanism, even if you developed a bad habit out of laziness and not due to an emotional issue, it will reinforce it and play it back over and over again. So in essence, you don't need to have some deep underlying issue in order to develop bad habits. The subconscious mind is simply doing its job. The irony is that if you developed a bad habit that is not backed by an emotional trauma, in time, the bad habit and its effects will CAUSE an emotional trauma. This sounds very negative, but the intent is not as bad as it may appear.

This book was written to rattle your subconscious mind in both covert and overt ways. It can help you break through and conquer those limiting beliefs so you can lessen or eliminate their control over your life. You will find that some issues will disappear immediately and some issues that will need a bit of work. In either case, you will feel a shift quickly.

For many, this will be a new process. This is, I admit, a journey into the unknown parts of your mind. I assure you; this process will help you understand yourself and some of the patterns in your life that are holding you back. Of course, by law, I cannot guarantee results. However, I feel the shift you seek in your life will become a reality.

In Part 1 of this book you will learn some important background information before getting to the specific Meridian Tapping and Switchword exercises.

In this section, we will discuss the subconscious mind and brain mechanisms that are relevant to this topic. We will also discuss Meridian Tapping and Switchwords in more detail.

In part 2, we will put the pieces together and jump headlong into a few exercises and how they can be used to initiate change in various aspects of your life…

Let us start from the beginning.

CHAPTER 1: THE SUBCONSCIOUS MIND

Often when people think about the subconscious mind they conjure up images of a mysterious subterranean landscape shrouded in an inky, impenetrable darkness. In that darkness lurks all our deepest and darkest secrets and desires. It also contains the keys to great spiritual light and wisdom we are all trying to tap into. We are told that it is wise beyond anything we can imagine and that by tapping into it we can reveal wonderful and powerful things about ourselves. We are also told that if you have repressed issues this same aspect of mind can destroy your life.

All that is true, but I would like to say that it is probably not as mysterious as it may appear. To reinforce the notion that it is too mysterious to understand will perpetuate the lack of understanding further and lead people to believe that they can't really do anything about their bad habits and thoughts. The subconscious mind has a practical and positive purpose. I will try to demystify some of these elements. Much of it is a mystery I cannot argue with that.

However, we can have some understanding of how it works and how we can use it to change things around.
The subconscious mind has several characteristics, I won't go into every single one of them, but here are a few that are relevant to our discussion.

- It controls everything you aren't actively thinking about.
- It has a perfect memory.
- It has only your best in mind.
- It has no discernment between real and unreal events.
- It always gets its way.
- It loves Consistency.

It controls everything you aren't actively thinking about.

The subconscious mind on a practical level controls everything you are not consciously thinking about or are aware of. For example, I am sure as you read this you are not consciously controlling your breathing, heart rate and all the myriad functions that are necessary for life. Maybe through meditation and mindfulness you might be able to control your breathing and your heart rate, but it is much harder to consciously control the millions upon millions of chemical and cellular reactions that are taking place in your body right this second. Harder still is it to keep track of all the molecular and atomic reactions that are taking place for those chemicals and cellular actions to even take place in the first place.

It's mind boggling how many processes are taking place just at the moment it takes you to read this sentence alone. These processes run smoothly because of the subconscious mind. This fact alone is testament to how powerful this part of your mind is. If you take a moment to fathom this, you will be in awe at how complex it all is. What is ironic about this is that even though you are not consciously controlling all these elements of your existence, it is still you. It's a part of you that you do not have full conscious control over.

If you could tap into even a fraction of this power, it can and will change everything for you...For better or for worse.

The Subconscious minds control extends across all functions of your being, not just your body. It also exerts a tremendous amount of control on your psychological state as well.

Have you ever had thoughts that race like a runaway train that is about to collide with an oil truck?
Have you ever had feelings of sadness creep up on you for no reason whatsoever?
What triggered those thoughts?

The mental health professional will say it is just a chemical reaction in the brain (we will briefly go into brain mechanisms later in this book). Just like the beating of your heart, the subconscious mind controls it by initiating these chemical responses. It is not magical in any way. The intangible subconscious mind is moving the tangible material chemical processes. Calling these negative thoughts a brain chemistry malfunction or subconscious control doesn't matter, the results are the same. Whenever you have a repetitive thought or compulsion that you can't seem to control, that is your subconscious mind compelling you. Although the subconscious mind is the repository of all wisdom, it isn't particularly mindful of proper etiquette when it is trying to convey this wisdom; it can drive you mad...literally. This irony exists throughout the brain. The brain is the center of the nervous system and communicates the pain and pleasure sensations perfectly, yet the brain itself doesn't have the capacity to actually feel pleasure or pain. The brain "KNOWS" that drugs and alcohol can damage it, but yet it is seemingly powerless to stop it, in fact the brain demands more of these toxins once you develop an addiction to them.

It's amusing that the brain, the seat of the intellect and self control can often exhibit very little intellectual capacity or self control. Yet despite these seeming weaknesses, great things also come from the brain and the subconscious mind. It's a paradox I do not think we will ever truly understand, but by observing how it works, we can use it to work in our lives in a beneficial way. As a side note, the brain and the subconscious mind cannot be separated neatly, I separate them to illustrate concepts, they are, in fact, intertwined.

I have read in several books that in order to reprogram the subconscious you have to "trick it". In reality, there is no tricking involved; it is simply reprogramming and tweaking the programmed behavior along the way. The term "trick" implies that you can use a conscious device to pull one over the subconscious mind; the reason this won't work is because your subconscious mind was introduced to your life events via your conscious mind and not the other way around. If you were traumatized, you weren't traumatized first subconsciously, rather you were traumatized first consciously and it moved into the subconscious mind for processing. So when we go about reprogramming the subconscious mind, we will be using the conscious mind to introduce the new program and tweaks. Not as a trick, but as a new program. Just like with a computer, the hard drive isn't created with the operating system already installed. Someone needed to install it. There is no tricking, just installing and tweaking.

One thing to remember is that although we can reprogram the subconscious mind, the old programming will always be archived, but this too can be used to empower us. It's a very good thing that the subconscious mind keeps all the bad habits in an archive. That archive serves as a reservoir of experience we can tap into. Imagine if you learned a skill but forgot it the moment you learned a newer one. Would that be very advantageous? Absolutely not, the old skill will always be valuable and that is why it is stored in your mental archive and not deleted entirely. If new skills and experiences were deleted by newer ones, we would be living every day as if it was our first day on earth. That would not be a pretty sight... This leads me to the next trait.

It has a perfect memory.

A few months ago, I was watching an episode of House MD, probably one of my most favorite shows on television. In this episode one of his patients had an ability that everyone coveted. She had a perfect memory. For some, it was like a magic trick when she recalled every detail. But this perfect memory had a debilitating dark side; she could never forget all the trauma she had experienced in her life.

She could "forgive" people with her words but she could never forget their actions and so it sabotaged her entire life. It's one thing to have a good memory for facts, figures and faces, but it is entirely another to have a perfect memory of your traumas, fears and pain. You would not be able to live in this world. Although you cannot recall everything consciously (which is a good thing), your subconscious mind has everything you have ever experienced saved in its database. If your mind suddenly inverted and the subconscious mind was fully conscious with all its memories, you would pretty much remember everything at once since the subconscious mind doesn't keep track of time in the conventional sense of the word. You wouldn't be able to use any of that memory because like in a dream, it may not always make sense. In either case, you would remember everything, from the moment you came out of the birth canal to just a second ago.

It is for this reason you can experience a past event right now in full detail. The subconscious mind cannot tell if this event happened just now or decades ago. The subconscious mind is like a sponge that never gets fully saturated in terms of its memory of events. Despite not being fully saturated, it has memory leaks into the conscious mind from time to time. These memory leaks may occur for no apparent reason, no apparent trigger is necessary. Something is squeezing that sponge and it starts leaking. It's for this reason you can suddenly recall traumatic events from early childhood without there being an apparent reason or trigger for those thoughts.

The Subconscious mind seems to be very adept at making us relive past traumas. There are several reasons why trauma is most often relived but pleasurable and happy events are not relived with the same frequency and intensity. Here are some points to remember about the subconscious minds use of memory.

• **Any event that is experienced that caused a substantial emotional response imprints immediately on to the subconscious mind.**
• **Pursuit of immediate pleasure has more impact in the short term, but often causes long term pain that endures if not addressed.**
• **Subconscious mind loves short term pleasure.**
• **Pain has more utility than pleasure when it comes to making changes in life.**
• **If you don't use pain wisely, it causes self sabotage and thus, more pain.**

As stated above, any event that is highly traumatic emotionally will imprint on the subconscious mind immediately. This also applies to pleasurable events as well; we have all had very intense emotional highs during happy times in our lives. Yet, we never seem to relive them with the same intensity as the bad ones. The pleasurable memories come and go; the bad ones seem to linger obsessively. I want to get into why the subconscious mind seems to only remember the bad events and not the good ones. Believe it or not, It's actually a good thing.

There is a principle called the 'pleasure-pain principle' and it is a perverse principle at that. Our desire for pleasure is often a need for instant gratification and avoidance of pain at all costs, at least in the short term. However, this often causes enduring long term pain. Advertising companies know this well and exploit this to make their quarterly earnings results. They don't care about the long term pain their products may inflict. That's your problem and it occasionally becomes theirs. Their profits outweigh most litigation that results from their lack of long term perspective.

Let's look at a scenario that illustrates the pleasure-pain principle: If you have weight to lose you know how hard it is to control food intake. Trust me; I know about this, it's tough but not insurmountable. Barring any hormonal or organic disease most of our weight gain is due to the compulsion to overeat, it's habitual. We know we shouldn't be eating that chocolate glazed donut. It looks so good doesn't it?

But we eat it anyway. Our need for pleasure in the movement outweighs the pain...but not for long.

What happens when you finish that donut?
Do you feel guilty?
Do you look in the mirror and reflect on your poor decision?
Has repeating this same compulsion made you feel self conscious in clothing?
Have you been rejected by people because of your weight?

If you answered yes to any of those questions, then you know how PAINFUL it is. Do those feelings last longer than the time it took to eat the donut? You bet they do. All it takes is one donut to cause all that pain. Now here is the problem, the subconscious mind is experiencing both emotions at once. It wants to give you pleasure so it makes you crave that donut right now. It also wants to avoid pain and wants you to be thin and healthy because it wants to avoid the feelings of insecurity that often accompanies weight gain. As you may know, the pain outlasts the pleasure long term.

As I mentioned earlier the brain/subconscious mind has paradoxical tendencies so it ignites both responses in an endless loop. I call it the Endless Loop of Insanity. That loop has to be broken. The pain you experience being overweight must outweigh the pleasure of having the donut in order to short circuit the endless loop of insanity. When this happens ,the subconscious mind will then make the donut appear as a danger to your wellbeing and you won't touch it. How does it do that? It links negative repulsive thoughts with the donuts because it perceives them as an immediate cause of the pain. Thus, it will reinforce good habits instead of bad ones in order to avoid the pain.

As you may have guessed, In order to do that it must utilize pain, not pleasure. The pleasure is utilized when you achieve your weight loss goals. Once this happens you have an endless loop occur once again, but in reverse. You will love exercising and hate the donut. I guess that positive loop can be called "The endless loop of sanity". The reason pain is used first in this scenario is because sometimes we have not experienced the pleasure of being thin so the subconscious mind can't reference it so it has to create pain in order to achieve pleasure. Of course, it doesn't actively know this.

Once it does though, you're on the right path. This also applies to addiction; notice that addicts feel pain when they stop taking their substance of choice at first. However, as the pleasure and benefits of being sober gains momentum, suddenly the tables turn, and sobriety becomes the preferred norm. Now if you don't change the negative habit, it will get reinforced and you will be compelled to self sabotage, this is why it is important to gain control ASAP. If you don't get out of the endless loop of insanity, you will go through endless pleasure-pain loops that will either force you to change or sadly, cause permanent pain in the long term.

I was stunned to learn all this and even more stunned to see the countless times I have done things to gain immediate pleasure only to inflict worse pain later because I did not handle the issue. Can you think of a time when you did this to yourself?

One caveat I would like to add is that in many cases pleasure is not what causes the loop initially, but pain. If a person is traumatized, the pain is what is experienced first, not pleasure (as in the case of the Donut). In this negative scenario what happens is it causes a kind of pain-pain loop. Suddenly thoughts of inadequacy arise which then cause you to sabotage relationships or other aspects of your life. But even this has a good intention although delivered in a painful package. In this case, pain becomes the norm, the subconscious mind thinks this pain is how it should be and thus you will continue to create negative situations to enforce the pain. So in a sense, the subconscious mind thinks it is "good". If it sees the same pattern all the time it faithfully creates an enduring pattern to perpetrate more of that. Like I mentioned, the subconscious mind is paradoxical in nature and sometimes perversely so. I assure you that despite these seemingly negative traits, the subconscious mind has a good intention; I will address this more in a bit.

Another reason the subconscious mind prompts you to relive traumatic events is because it is telling you that you need to deal with the issues that are underlying the trauma. Generally speaking, when good things happen to you, they don't produce negative and self sabotaging behavior. For the most part, they don't cause repression and suppression in the subconscious mind. The Subconscious mind stores them as "non-issues", there is no resolution needed. However, when there are unresolved issues, they will stay lodged in your subconscious mind until they are dealt with. This is actually a service to you.

This perfect memory as I stated before is a perfect sponge that never gets fully saturated, but that doesn't mean it doesn't leak on occasion. A leak no matter how slow, over time, can reshape even the hardest material. In terms of the subconscious mind, unresolved issues such as trauma can start dripping slowly into your conscious mind and all of a sudden an outburst of negative behavior and sabotaging actions take place. Unresolved anger can suddenly erupt into violence towards oneself or others. Unresolved issues of worthiness can cause you to spend all your money wastefully and without regard for tomorrow or overeat etc. I had to deal with these worthiness issues and it caused me to completely put myself into the poor house several times. It's only when I faced them that I was able to get my life back with plenty of room for improvement.

There are so many different toxic emotional leaks you could experience and it is all due to the subconscious minds perfect memory. I can imagine by now you want to reach into your psyche and surgically remove your subconscious mind. It sounds absolutely awful, I know. Besides the fact that it keeps you alive, It doesn't sound good at all, but really, it isn't as bad as it appears.

It has only your best in mind.

After everything I just said it would take a miracle for me to convince you that the subconscious mind could have anything else but malicious intent for your life. I am a man that believes in miracles. After reading this book, I have a feeling you will too.

So what exactly does "It has only your best in mind" mean?

When trauma occurs either in childhood or in adulthood, your mind, like your body during physical trauma develops scar tissue. Scar tissue doesn't always look pretty, but if you knew the intention of that scar tissue, you might start taking a shine to it. The scar tissue is an attempt to protect that part of your body so if such an event would occur again, it would result in less damage. In the mind, this scar tissue is called a defense mechanism.

If trauma is experienced and it is substantial, your mind will develop a defense mechanism in order to protect from trauma if such an event would occur again. Often these scars don't look pretty either. The immediate mental protection comes in the form of denial. There are, however, positive and negative forms of denial. Positive denial protects you from a current bad event so it doesn't completely overtake you, whereas negative denial feeds defense mechanisms. Positive denial, if not addressed after the trauma becomes negative denial and defense mechanisms sprout up like weeds.

Here is a good example of how a defense mechanism might unfold. Let's look at a scenario of a person who got hurt in a relationship or experienced a breakup and it traumatizes them badly. Often they find themselves single for long stretches of time because they are afraid to get hurt. Whenever they do manage to go on a date, they put up walls so they won't get hurt again. It's not even conscious, it's all unconscious; they want to be in a relationship but their thoughts and actions are controlled by the subconscious mind and they can't seem to break it. They can't break it, because they may not be fully conscious that this is what is going on. Remember, the subconscious is paradoxical and thinks it is protecting you but doesn't realize this protection often comes at a far higher price in the future. It wants protection now, forget about tomorrow.

I admit, this defense mechanism hits home for me, I have lived with this defense mechanism for a good deal of my adult life. I didn't just put up a wall; I rationalized until I was blue in the face as to why women wouldn't like me. When I wasn't fully convinced of that, I would rationalize to myself why I wouldn't like them. It all made perfect sense at the time. I rationalized my way to misery and isolation. **Rationalization is a powerful weapon of the mind because it is so seamlessly woven into your thought processes. You don't realize that it has hijacked your better judgment. It's for this reason we all can self sabotage so easily and completely and not realize we are doing so.** It hit me like a demolition ball when I finally realized what was going on.

My experience is a good but a tame example of self sabotage and a defense mechanism at play. Although defense mechanisms are potentially dangerous, there is beauty in such a mechanism because it is so automatic and paradoxical. When it is engaged, it makes so much sense in the moment. We can't even see the possibility that it is a defense mechanism when it is occurring. It's only in retrospect that we realized that we "screwed everything up". This retrospective realization doesn't help unless it prompts you to make a change. If you are not prompted to change, it just adds an extra layer of reinforcement aka guilt and shame to the wall you have up, and thus fortifying it for when it gets in a situation when it is engaged again. There are TONS of examples that can illustrate how this process works.

From what I have just written it seems very hard to fathom that there is a good intention there. I would like to parse through the above example to illustrate why the defense mechanism has good intentions. The result may not be optimal, but it did its job. The subconscious has no idea that the defense mechanism is a bad idea. It is only trying to protect you from getting hurt NOW. When I got hurt very badly by a breakup, my intention wasn't to crawl under a rock and never date again, but the pain of it kept me away from dating for a while. The pain of the breakup was so intense, my subconscious kicked in and said (figuratively speaking) "Wow this really hurt; I need to protect myself from going through this pain again". Then when I did date again I had every excuse and rationalization in the book to not date. The defense mechanism must protect you from this pain at all costs and as a result, your thought process will get twisted in order for this to happen. In many ways the subconscious mind it is like a child, it jumps headlong into something and doesn't always think it through. So in a sense the subconscious mind is "id-ridden". So in an attempt to safeguard me from the future heart break, it armed me to the teeth so that if there was any possibility of pain, I could easily shoot it down with -myself sabotaging behaviors, thus insuring no one would date me long term or I would rationalize and find a reason not to date them. It still shocks me at how seamlessly rationalizations can enter the thought process.

In many ways a defense mechanism is like an overactive immune system of the mind. The problem is, even the immune system, if it is unregulated and goes into hyper drive will start attacking the body. The germ it intended to target might be eradicated long ago, but now your organs are the target. The same thing occurs with a defense mechanism, when engaged, it protects you from the harm it was intended to protect you from, but if it is not immediately taken down or adjusted once the threat has passed ,the supplies you need to survive will not get through. That Great Wall of China you built stays up. So as you can see, the INTENT of the subconscious mind to protect is pure, in fact, it could not be purer. It is just a tad too eager to protect you. Do defense mechanisms work? In my case it sure did at the time. I never got hurt by a woman again, but I had to deal with years of loneliness in order to achieve that. The subconscious did its job well and with a pure "heart" but it didn't know the consequences of that intention. It's that pesky paradoxical nature at play again. If you take a moment to think how this might relate to your life, you will find this will probably hold true for you as well. As I mentioned earlier, the subconscious is like a child and like children, you need to guide them so they make better decisions. Mold your subconscious mind, otherwise it will mold you.

It has no discernment between real and unreal events.

The subconscious mind has a powerful strength that may seem like a weakness. It has no discernment between real and unreal events, places or things. When the subconscious mind processes information, it assumes it is all real, that is unless the new information bumps up against an entrenched repetitive pattern or belief. This is very important to remember. The subconscious mind categorizes information using different emotional weights. If the information is backed up by emotion, that information will practically fossilize in the subconscious mind. This aspect intrigues me the most because it is counter to how we consciously process information. Example: I am pretty confident in my knowledge that there is no such thing as a Pegasus (A flying horse). The subconscious mind however has no way of knowing this. If I don't believe in a Pegasus, how can the subconscious mind then take that information and believe in them?

That is because the subconscious doesn't make judgments on the veracity of the information it is given unless it bumps up against an entrenched repetitive thought or pattern. It is for all intents and purposes a recording device, a very stubborn one at that.

Here is a scenario proving this. Have you ever had a dream that seemed so real that your body actually responded to it? Such as a falling dream, or a sad dream that made you cry when you woke up? Notice how the body reacted; it reacted as if it was a real event. Your subconscious mind is most "itself" when it is in the dream state and so it thinks the content of the dream is so real that it tells the body to respond as if it were an actual event taking place in waking consciousness. If it knew the difference between actually falling down and falling down in a dream, you wouldn't grip the bed as if you were falling. The fact the subconscious mind makes you react like you are actually falling is proof positive it has no conception at all of reality.

I can imagine that after reading all this you might be shocked that the wellspring of all wisdom could be... how shall I say ...so stupid. Well, that is a valid thought, but I want to clarify that the subconscious mind is not stupid, it's paradoxical and lacks context.

It's this lack of context that allows us to mold it to our benefit or to our detriment. Think of the subconscious mind as a car, it has no context, it has only pure potential. It can go 1 mile an hour or 150 miles an hour. It can rush you to the hospital or be the reason you are going to the hospital in the first place. It's pure potential power, YOU have to give it context and direction. Otherwise the car will just simply move in the direction of least resistance. What happens when you put a car in neutral on a hill? It will go wherever gravity is pulling it. The subconscious mind is the same, it will gravitate towards repetition and patterns you set for it. It has all the wisdom you can possibly imagine, but if it is not directed, it will control your life and you will call it fate. Remember Carl Jung's quote?

Countless studies have been done to prove the subconscious mind has no sense of reality. Athletes, Astronauts and many more have used this to their advantage for decades. It has been called Visual Motor Rehearsal. Like a dream, you are enacting something without actually doing it in real life. You are simply visualizing it. It has been proven that by just using your senses to imagine yourself doing a particular sport or activity; the required muscles will start reacting as if you were really performing this activity. As I stated before, the subconscious is responsible for the body's activities. You aren't actually moving a muscle, your body is completely reacting to your thoughts and the subconscious mind is making sure the reactions that occur behind the scenes are in play and are activated. Now the conscious mind knows full well you aren't actually performing this activity, but the subconscious mind has no clue and starts firing on all cylinders as if you were really performing the activity. This is because the conscious mind is using all senses to visualize this.

There was an interesting study further illustrating how the subconscious mind takes much of what it filters as actual and real. Melissa Bateson and colleagues at Newcastle University, UK conducted an experiment at their psychology department coffee room. In the coffee room, faculty were encouraged to have as much coffee and tea as they like. This system was run using an "Honesty Box". This box collected money for the coffee and tea that was provided for the faculty. Although it was not "mandatory" to leave money, it is a courteous practice to do so. Above the honesty box they placed a nice picture of flowers and a suggested price list. At the end of the week money was collected and counted. However, the following week the picture was not that of flowers, but of a pair of eyes staring right at the person who happens to be in front of the "honesty box" at the time. The faces changed, but the eyes were always staring, directly at the person in front of the "Honesty box". Although the pair of eyes was just a photocopy of actual eyes, the faculty reacted unconsciously to those eyes as if they were real. How do we know? The weeks that the pictures of the eyes were present, more money was collected. In fact 2.76 times more money was collected during the weeks the eyes were above the "Honesty Box". Although this study was to measure "honesty" and the various subliminal cues involved in producing honest behavior, it also illustrates to me that the subconscious mind prompts behavior based on stimuli it perceives as real. If the subconscious mind truly knew that the image of the pair of eyes was not an actual set of eyes, it wouldn't have prompted unconscious behavior indicating the opposite. This study can be found in Biology Letters (DOI: 10.1098/rsbl.2006.0509).

This information has been covered in other books but I believe they do not utilize this principle properly. Other books recommend using this aspect of the subconscious mind by telling you to "fake it till you make it". If all this is true, it should work considering the subconscious mind cannot tell the difference between the real and unreal, right? But yet, "fake it till you make it" fails more often than it works. Why is this so? "Fake it till you make it" doesn't always work because it is bumping up against an entrenched and ingrained pattern of belief or behavior. You have probably used affirmations and visualization to reprogram your mind and have failed to see the results you were expecting. If the subconscious mind has no conception of reality, these affirmations should have elicited the same real visceral responses like you would have in a dream or visual motor rehearsal, but they didn't. I have experienced the same thing and that is one of the reasons people have started looking at visualizations and affirmations in a negative light. It simply doesn't work as easily as all these books state it does. I wish it did.

As I mentioned above, the subconscious mind loves repetition and patterns, if you have an ingrained habit and all you have been doing is reinforcing it, the subconscious mind will invalidate all those affirmations because it has no proof that those old habits should be abandoned. Chanting affirmations alone is not considered proof. The subconscious mind needs a bit more. For example, If you replace drinking with running for a few weeks and then start saying "I am a great runner", then the subconscious mind will most likely be receptive to the affirmation. This is because the affirmation will no longer be bumping up against an old repetitive pattern.

In order to help yourself replace old habits you must reduce some of the emotional charge behind the current habit. The fact that a particular aspect you want to change is carrying such a huge emotional charge for you is the very key to why it can't just be replaced so quickly with a new program. That emotional charge is what is giving it energy. The key to installing new programming is to reduce the amplitude of the emotional charge stemming from the behavior or image you are trying to change. If it still has a high emotional charge, the subconscious mind will not let it go. Remember, it believes that it is trying to protect you. The techniques presented in this book will help you clear out the emotional charge for the thing you want to change so you can install a new program. Other programs have called it "getting clear". I will provide you with tools that will get you clear on several levels at once.

It always gets its way.

As I mentioned, the subconscious mind loves repetition. In fact, I will repeat this fact over and over again because that is the best way to learn. This is a very critical element of the subconscious mind that we need to focus on the most. The fact that the subconscious mind always gets its way is the reason why we are often stuck in our repetitive self sabotaging patterns. If we do not reprogram or override the subconscious mind with new programming, the old program will continue to play and until it is tweaked or uninstalled, the subconscious mind will continue to drive you to perform the old habits. It will succeed almost every time. It always gets its way. This is why it has been historically difficult for people to change. The old program is still running, sure it can go into the background but after a while it starts draining your resources and you will be forced to either cave into it or use it to advance yourself to a better place.

I know all this sounds very mechanical. In actuality, it is very much like that. We do not have to look very far to see that our body operates in a very mechanical way. I assure you that as we get deeper into the book we will start moving into the realm of the spiritual and abstract. At first we want to start from the ground up. Let's deal with the gears first and work our way up. In reality it is all spiritual, but often I find going up a ladder one step at a time and using the appropriate terminology for each step is a great way to understand the grand scheme of things.

Back to the subconscious mind: the subconscious wants its way or the highway. It will have temper tantrums until it gets what it wants, which means you will have the tantrum at the worst possible time. I have read countless self help books and many of them do not truly address the methods the subconscious uses to get what it wants. The primary methods or defense mechanisms are Suppression, Repression, Displacement, Projection, Psychosomatic disease; these are perfect measures for how the subconscious mind controls us. These 5 concepts are very important in understanding why the subconscious always gets its way and why it gets its way in such a dramatic fashion and often so covertly you do not even know it is happening. Then there is a subgroup of symptoms that emanate from the defense mechanism process. These are easier to identify because they can be discerned almost immediately as they occur.

This Subgroup expresses itself through the following ways:
- **Procrastination and Escapism**
- **Cynicism - Being Jaded**
- **Negative Thinking**
- **Negative Skepticism**
- **Defeatism**

Often, many self help books will tell you that the moment you have a negative thought or feel the need to indulge in copious amounts of cake, you must immediately think about something else. This works for a while, but it is not a solution. After a short time the old behavior rebounds and not only does that person indulge in the cake, they are virtually eating up the entire bakery. This of course applies to other areas of life as well. I am willing to wager that this method hasn't really worked for anyone long term. Has it worked for you? Probably not, that's why you have purchased this book. You can't suppress those negative feelings, it doesn't work. To consciously suppress these things is like building a dam with holes in it. Sure it keeps most of the water out; that is until the holes get larger and the whole structure breaks apart and viola, you are swept away by the current. (In the above example that would be equivalent to eating the entire bakery.)

Many of these methods are only placing bubble gum in those leaking holes. They can't hold back that torrent.

Another popular piece of advice that is given is to not think about the bad events in your life and by not thinking about them, they eventually fade. As they say, "time heals all wounds". I used to believe that, but I do not any longer. It might work for small disappointments, but not trauma. Forgetting the event or REPRESSING IT won't get rid of it either. Thoughts and feeling that are buried alive will never ever die. You may think they are dead because you haven't thought about them in a while, but I assure you, they are stirring underneath, running your life in such subtle ways that you don't even realize how much control they have over you.. It's like a scene in a horror film when naive, carefree teenagers decide to break into a cemetery because it's cool. Then suddenly... a hand emerges from one of the graves and tries to grab one of them to their doom. The repressed emotion and issue will emerge like that too, unexpectedly, and in an awfully frightening way. When you commit an act of self sabotage that shocks even you, that is most likely the result of a repressed issue that has decided to rise from the grave. If you suppress and repress emotions and issues long enough, and the subconscious finally wants to get your attention, it will often operate under Murphy's Law. What can go wrong will go wrong and at the worst possible time. Have you ever experienced that before? Have you ever found yourself saying "I DON'T NEED THIS IN MY LIFE RIGHT NOW?" "GOD, WHAT WAS I THINKING?" "HOW COULD I HAVE DONE THAT?"… Take heed.

Another sly way the subconscious mind tries to communicate with you is through displacement. Displacement occurs when an unacceptable thought, idea, emotion or impulse stirring in the subconscious mind is perceived to be dangerous or painful. So to dissipate the pain, it goes on and redirects to something that appears to be more acceptable and less threatening. A simple example of displacement is punishing a punching bag when you are angry. You certainly won't go and punch your friend in the face (although you may really want to), so you displace that anger by punching a punching bag. Have you ever had a bad day and then take it out on others who had nothing to do with it? I think we all have; that's displacement in one of its uglier forms.

Projection is another incredibly common defense mechanism that I think we all have displayed on many occasions. This is a particular hard one to deal with because it is so pervasive and so damaging; not only to the person who is projecting, but to the people or person they are projecting upon. When we have undesired impulses ,thoughts and motivations and refuse to deal with them, we often go out of our way and accuse other people of having and acting on those same desires and having those same thoughts and flaws.

For example, the person who comes across as perfect and criticizes others for not being perfect are often harboring in their own psyche that same imperfection or an internal perception

34

that they themselves are imperfect. They can't deal with it, so they project it onto others. Or a more common example is how we react to the tabloids. Have you ever read the tabloids and read how movie stars are ruining their lives with either alcohol or drug addiction? Or perhaps they gain weight and we immediately say "What a train wreck" or "wow, she sure gained a lot of weight, look how fat she is". Of course the same person saying this suddenly doesn't seem to notice that they too have a few pounds to lose and probably have a bad habit or two they need to break. These thoughts are too painful for them to truly accept so they are quick to point out the same flaws in others. I have noticed this several times at the supermarket.

I hear people pointing out how fat some actress has become, it's often ironic because the person making the criticism is in line and about to pay for a bucket of ice cream and a 6 pack of beer. Mind you, the beer is never of the "light" variety.

Notice that this behavior is completely unconscious and automatic. Just because the anxiety has been displaced or projected doesn't mean the issue has been resolved, it just gave short term pleasure and relief in the moment. It simply becomes an excuse not to deal with it. A person suddenly rationalizes and says, "My problem pales in comparison, they have it much worse than I do, it certainly won't cause that much damage in my life." This line of reasoning almost forgives the bad behavior and makes it somehow less of an issue. The thing is, it doesn't, and it's just as damaging to your life as it is for the stars. It's just more public for them.

Displacement and projection keep you stuck. Both Displacement and Projection and the other defense mechanisms are the root cause of much hypocrisy and judgment in the world. Jesus Knew this well when he said "How can you say to your brother, 'Let me take the speck out of your eye,' when all the time there is a plank in your own eye?"

None of us are immune to the subconscious minds "wrath". In my case, I always had a clean bill of health throughout the time I drank heavily. I thought to myself "I am not like those drinkers who get all out of control and unhealthy". I used to shake my head when I saw drunk and addicted people. Not realizing that if I looked in the mirror , I was drunk and addicted too. Passing judgment made me feel better and made me feel resilient. Of course I also didn't notice the extra 20 lbs I was carrying. I was oblivious, that is until one Easter Sunday when I drank myself into oblivion, threw away some of my belongings, cried and screamed out of control and stumbled around like a drunkard. It wasn't my best moment for sure. To top it all off, the results came back from the latest blood work at the time and a serious elevation in a key chemical that is a factor for heart disease was present. They also found arthritic degeneration in my neck that as the doctor said " Is not seen in your age group." You can bet I am sober now and 20 lbs lighter.

I drink only on social occasions but I never drink alone or to that level ever. Switchwords had a HUGE hand in this transformation. I would not have been able to do it without them.

These defense mechanisms above cause us to commit outrageous and countless acts of self sabotage and hypocrisy. For example: There are people who crusade against a certain idea or behavior only to be found committing those same behaviors. You do not have to look far to find high profile people who rail against prostitution only to be caught with their pants down soliciting a prostitute. Or a minister who rails against homosexuality only to find out that he has engaged in a homosexual relationship FOR YEARS. Or the person rallying against drugs, only to be caught buying them and is hopelessly addicted to them. Defense mechanism can show in all sorts of ways that cause us to live inauthentic lives. These defense mechanisms can become so painful it can cause a person to commit suicide. One example I read recently was about a young, attractive, educated woman in NYC who lead a flawless and happy life, she had an ideal life by any standard. One early morning, she jumps to her death in an apparent suicide.

What about the person who wins the lottery only to go broke and deeply in debt in a short period of time? These examples can be found in the news every single day. And it is found in our lives as well. If you think for a moment, you may come up with quite a few examples of this in your own life.
The fifth way the subconscious mind can communicate when it is desperate to get through to you is through psychosomatic pain and disease. Have you ever known a person who always complains of aches and pains or thinks they are sick, but time after time the doctors can't find anything wrong with them? What did you say to that person? " ITS ALL IN YOUR HEAD". A truer statement has never been made. BUT the common misconception of such a statement is that it is not real. IT IS VERY REAL; the origins of the discomfort however, can't be conventionally measured. You can't take a blood test for phantom pain, at least not that I know of. It is no wonder that pharmaceutical companies have created new antidepressants that also target this phantom pain. In one commercial it states

"depression hurts". What's funny about these medications is that in the inserts it states that the mechanism through which these drugs work is not yet understood. That is because it is not entirely chemical, there is a spiritual aspect working as well.

Psychosomatic illness and pain strikes more people than you can imagine. I should know, from 1996-2001, I was stricken with phantom pain (I was a ball of defense mechanisms firing on all cylinders). I had just gotten back from overseas after a breakup. I was still mourning the loss of that relationship, I never truly dealt with it and as the subconscious is want to do, it buried the pain and slowly formed scar tissue. I just felt the grief but didn't work through it. Suddenly in February of 1996, I was stricken with this odd and VERY painful sensation in my lower extremities. So painful in fact it ruined any hope for a romantic or social life. (The pain stopped me from having meaningful relationships. Why? The subconscious mind was protecting me from rejection). Doctor after doctor said the same thing "I don't know what is wrong with you, but here, take this and let's see what happens." "This" meaning antibiotics, analgesics, you name it. I was on antibiotics for an infection I never had and was on them for YEARS. It had to have taken years off my life I am sure. I was poked and prodded and they found nothing.

One doctor told me "you are just going to have to deal with it." I was in my early to mid 20s; you want to destroy a young man in the prime of his life, that's what you tell him. I eventually stopped working and spiraled downhill.

I did a lot of soul searching and praying during that time. I eventually found a doctor (who is still my doctor to this day) who changed my perception. The doctor told me this was psychosomatic…He was right. Ever since this revelation, I have been pain free. That was 12 years ago… how time flies. A combination of various modalities and therapy cured it right up, never to return. This pain taught me a very important lesson; feelings you bury alive and ignore will come back to haunt you until you are brought to your knees. Some people stay on their knees and others, LIKE YOU, are getting back up.

Some mainstream doctors have started to come around to the idea that psychosomatic illnesses are real. They have started to suggest that almost all chronic pain not directly tied to a physiological problem may very well be psychosomatic. It's not surprising that Meridian tapping, a component of this book has such a high success rate dealing with psychosomatic illness. It is VERY useful in unraveling psychosomatic pain. Psychosomatic pain if not treated over the long term can actually result in the production of a tangible condition and so it is imperative to deal with it as soon as possible. By law, I do need to state that this book is not a replacement for medical and psychological care. Please use these techniques reasonably and responsibly. This also leads me to state that for many; using these techniques has allowed them to attract the right mode of care that they needed. Suffice it to say, it is very powerful. Now we will cover the final aspect of the subconscious mind that is pertinent to this book. After that we will deal with the more obvious subgroups of symptoms you may encounter.

It loves Consistency.

One would think that if all this pain is being experienced, why isn't it easier to stop these negative behaviors? We are, after all, trying to avoid pain right?

The simple answer is IT'S COMFORTABLE, ITS SAFE, ITS FAMILIAR and IT DOESN'T HURT ENOUGH. Have you or do you know a person who leaves one abusive relationship only to get into another one? That's a symptom of the subconscious mind keeping you comfortably and securely in your comfort zone. It may seem like a bad relationship would be the epitome of discomfort, but if that is all you know, even the pain of that relationship becomes safe and RELIABLE. The subconscious mind loves consistency.

I experienced this first hand many years ago. I was really enamored with this wonderful woman, she was attractive, smart and we had great chemistry. I figured we would take it to the next level and become a "couple", instead she tells me "You are too good for me, I can't be in this relationship, I will screw it up". (She didn't use the word screw). You see? I was not what she was used to, she wanted a guy who would treat her poorly, and I gathered this because every relationship she ever talked about was with abusive men. She wasn't comfortable with me because I did not offer the same element of abuse she was used to. Later I discovered she had a string of relationships with abusive men and married and divorced several of them. Do you see a pattern here? This book will show you how to undo the negative consistencies in your life and replace them with new better thoughts and behaviors...Keep reading.

CHAPTER 2 CHRONIC SYMPTOMS OF SELF SABOTAGE

In the previous chapter we covered the broader defense mechanisms. Now we will discuss more overt symptoms that plague our everyday lives. I have dedicated a chapter to these symptoms because these are the more obvious emanations of the defense mechanism process. They are, in many ways, the chronic symptoms, whereas in the previous chapter we discussed the more acute ones.

These chronic symptoms are:
• **Procrastination and Escapism**
• **Cynicism - Being Jaded**
• **Negative thinking**
• **Negative Skepticism**
• **Defeatism**

Procrastination and Escapism

Procrastination is a very effective dream killer. Procrastination and escapism are one and the same. You want to escape something you don't want to do or deal with. When the spirit of procrastination possesses you, suddenly all these rationalizations emerge. Here is just one way I have been possessed by it. There was a time when I wanted to find a new job on Wall Street. In order for me to start applying I needed to buy a new suit, the problem was that I thought I looked horrible in a suit because of the weight I gained. So I told myself" I can't look for a job until I get a suit and I can't get the suit until I lose the weight". Ok, I cut myself some slack, I figured I can take two months and lose the weight. Unfortunately, my intention was not quite in line with my actions. Every day I said to myself "I will start my diet tomorrow". The problem is, tomorrow never came. What should have taken me two months never got done. In fact I stayed at the same job I wanted to leave for an additional two years. That is how powerful procrastination is. It is TASK AVERSION. I dreaded the work required to make the changes and I had fears that I would not be successful if I did get a new job.

In order to make meaningful change in your life it is important to be cognizant of what your particular issue is. Sometimes this requires you to face the demon you are trying so very hard to avoid. The Meridian tapping component of this program has the reputation of causing people to face these demons, sometimes this causes them to feel a great weight has lifted off their chests. Sometimes it can cause people to feel more anxious about it. But this anxiety is good, it means the issue is bubbling over and can now be addressed.

However, most people (including myself) are afraid of the demons, so instead we find a distraction. Something that will help us ESCAPE from these problems. For me, it was alcohol and frozen pizza. I admit, I still love frozen pizza, especially made by Amy's, it's delicious. But now I treat it as a meal and not as medication. If it is within my calorie budget, I eat it, if not, I don't. Escapism pops its head in very sinister ways because it is a seamless thought. Unless you are mindful, you may not catch it. When you are faced with a task you do not want to do your mind may say " Sure, I need to do this , but let's skip it, don't worry, we can go back to it later, or even better, why not sit in front of the TV and catch up on all the shows that

I recorded?"

Your dreams can be put off indefinitely so long as you are possessed by procrastination. The sinister result of procrastination is that the longer you give in to it, the more and more complacent you will become. The more complacent you become, the more distance between you and your goals. You don't want this to happen. The more distance between you and your goal, the less likely you will be motivated to take the actions necessary to achieve them. The clock will continue to tick away and as you move away from the goal, the clock ticks even faster. You will blink your eyes and a year will pass and you will be dumbfounded and think "Where did the time go?" My friend, once the time is gone, it is gone.

There is a very effective way to beat procrastination and that is through pain. But why go that route? Do you really need to have a heart attack before you start a fitness program? Do you really need to go broke before you save for tomorrow? No doubt, pain will motivate you, but there is a more effective way to bypass this and that is by using the principles in this book. They do work and have worked for so many people. Just search online and you will see what people are saying about them. Once you apply what you will learn, I have a feeling procrastination will soon be a thing of the past. I know it has for me.

Cynicism - Being Jaded

Cynicism is a scourge upon the land. This alone can produce the right environment for procrastination to occur. A Cynic is a person who is constantly judging and questioning the goodness and positivity of everything. They are the kind of people that will find a flaw in everything they encounter. This might be good in the corporate world where you need someone to be able to spot flaws in a very important project. But this doesn't work in day to day living. Sure, I think it is very important to observe your life and question certain things to make sure you are on track, but to me, that is just being mindful. The cynic however will find the flaw and then magnify it much larger than it already is. By making it larger, there is then less inclination to do anything about the flaw because it is suddenly "too big" to handle. When this happens, guess what happens next? Procrastination and escapism.

A cynic can never be truly happy because the joy they feel will be outweighed by the negativity experienced picking out the flaws. They are essentially jaded. Here is a good example that I am sure one of you out there might be thinking "I can't change my life by reading a book on Switchwords, whatever the hell they are". That is cynicism.

The cynic's thoughts are so intertwined with their experience that they can't even allow the possibility that they are wrong. If they are proven wrong, they will twist it in such a way that they look right. If you are cynic and you want to be right, just realize you will also remain stuck in the mud. A cynic will never allow for anything to work for them because they discount it before they even start. This is a killer of dreams. A Cynic may have big dreams but they will never fulfill them because they will find a flaw in everything, in every step of the way. The cure for a cynic is an open mind. Yes, all things have flaws, yes, this may not work for you. Give it a shot. Don't be so cynical :).

Negative thinking

As you may know, the number one problem to have when you are trying to make changes in life is negative thinking. A negative attitude has the power to undermine even the most well intended efforts because it is seamlessly woven into your thoughts and makes a lot of sense when it starts chattering away in your mind. "Why bother?" it says. "You know you don't have the self discipline to change, why even try?"

All this self talk is negative, negative thinking is in many ways related to cynicism because it dwells on what can go wrong. In some cases negative thinking is the result of years of being disappointed in life. I know in my own life that every time I failed another notch of negative thinking was etched into my mind. After awhile almost everything to me was negative. When negativity and cynicism encounter one another it sucks the life right out of you. You won't take chances in life because you are convinced you will fail. You won't start a diet because you have failed in the past. You won't ask that person out because you have been rejected before. Do you see how this is working? This negativity is a result of defense mechanism trying to protect you from future pain but at the expense of future gain.

Take heed, what I am about to say is very important. The subconscious mind can be very sly and often masquerades negative thinking as caution. When you think of negative thinking as being cautious, you give yourself a way out of making changes in your life. You will say " I am not being negative, I am simply being cautious". That, my friend, is hogwash. Yes, it is wise to exert caution in some cases but in most cases we don't need to be on guard as often as we think we do. Being on guard all the time is a symptom of negative thinking. 'The world is a dangerous place I must protect myself'. But what about all the beautiful things in life? You won't be able to experience them if you have a negative disposition.

Another sly way the subconscious mind keeps you negative is by convincing you that being negative is just "how you are". Implying that it is in some way a character trait you were born with. You weren't born a negative thinker. You were programmed to be one; whether it was conscious or not. Today, after you apply the principles in this book you will realize just how much control you do have over your attitudes and thought process.

Negative Skepticism

This is also a common symptom of a defense mechanism, it is very much related to negative thinking but it doesn't always have a negative outcome. There are positive forms of skepticism. A good time to exert skepticism is when you read the emails in your spam folder. Have you ever received emails stating that you are the beneficiary of a multimillion dollar account based in Africa or China? Have you received several of these emails from different people stating the same thing? Wow, you must have a lot of rich relatives and connections in Africa and China. They chose you to be the inheritor of all this money...JACKPOT BABY!!! Then, after you send them an email laying claim to your money they suddenly need you to send them money first. I don't need to tell you that the above scenario would surely warrant skepticism wouldn't you agree? I am not about to give my personal information to some dethroned Queen in exile who I don't even know so she can send me millions of dollars that her dictator husband left behind. Would you? If you would, well, I have beach front property in Iowa for you to buy. :)

In the above scenario, it is clear, skepticism is useful. It's when it starts getting in the way of you making changes is when it is detrimental. Like negative thinking, negative skepticism prevents you from fully looking at the broader picture, it prevents you from entertaining the notion that something could actually work for you. Like the techniques in this book for example. If you are like me, you read quite a bit of self help literature. There are so many techniques and "stuff" out there that it is very easy to grow skeptical about all the claims. If any of it worked there would be no need for other techniques right? Well, yes and no. Certain techniques work well for others but not for all. That's just the nature of the world. As they say " one man's trash is another man's treasure." It's like that in all areas of life. Now, I am not saying buy every new book that comes out. However, what I am saying is don't discount it right away. There could be a hidden gem there for you. Since I know the power of skepticism, it is for this reason I offered a 30 day money back guarantee when you purchased this e-book. It allows you to engage in healthy skepticism, not negative skepticism and with no risk. I find that both Meridian Tapping and Switchwords help open the mind in ways that you will find that you can entertain ideas that may very well revolutionize your life. Keep an open mind, it might open the doors of opportunity.

Defeatism

This symptom is very much related to all the others. It's a form of negative thinking but with deeper emotional connotations. Often we feel defeated in life when things don't go our way. At first this might be a natural consequence of feeling bad about a defeat. That's okay, it happens. Our confidence gets shaken when things don't work out, that's natural and usually not a big problem. It's when these defeats happen more often that we can develop defeatism. A defeated person is a person who has already lost the competition before they even entered. For example, when I was training for the J.P Morgan corporate challenge which is a 3.50 mile run, I had tons of doubts, some even self defeating. I thought to myself "You never ran that fast or for that amount of time ever, you may as well not even try." I almost caved into that feeling, but I didn't. In fact, Switchwords were the NUMBER 1 modality I used to get me through the run. I use them on every run to keep up my energy levels. Not only did I finish the run, I did the best time I ever would have dreamed to make. Now I run regularly and break all my personal records and I love it. Why am I telling you all this? I am doing so because if I would have caved into those defeating thoughts, I wouldn't have achieved what I did. it may not be a lot , but it was huge for me. Do you have a goal you are talking yourself out of?

Are any of the reasons of the "you can't" variety? If so, that's defeatism. It's your subconscious mind's way of protecting you from another disappointment. If you cave in to it, you will simply be reinforcing the defeating behavior. We need to change that around today. You won't allow yourself to be defeated again...right?

In the last two chapters we covered how subconscious beliefs are running our lives. We covered how and why we are completely unaware of it (Until now). Repressing the feelings won't work; they will just erupt like a volcano. Suppressing them certainly doesn't either because it will slowly erode our personal strength. Displacement doesn't work because it will boomerang right back at us. Procrastination, being a cynic etc destroys our daily experience of life. It must change NOW, the old ways of dealing with these issues doesn't work anymore.

So what does work?

The first step is acknowledging these self limiting thoughts and making peace with them, in other words, you don't want to deny them and you don't want to act them out, but what you want to do is look at them and acknowledge them; once you do that, you can start to clear them.

As Carl Jung said, "What you resist persists" and to add to the quote from conversations with God "what you look at, disappears". Meaning, its impact on you will diminish or go away when you acknowledge and deal with them. They will never be erased entirely, they will be archived, but that doesn't mean you can't reprogram your subconscious mind against the toxic effects of those old limiting beliefs. Some of your issues will vanish right away and some will take some time. I urge you to stick with it. Think of this program as a vaccine, the virus is not "dead" it is being kept in check by the antibodies that the vaccine helps your body produce. By knowing the past programming, it will help you avoid having it control you in the future. This book is about taking control over your subconscious mind and completely turning things in another direction. Although I stressed all the negatives about how the subconscious controls your life, it can also do the exact opposite and make your life a heaven on earth and that's what you and I are working towards in this book.

I really feel and believe that if we can reframe the way we look at the subconscious mind and self sabotage, the easier it is for us to change. Your conscious mind is a part of you just as much as the subconscious mind is. It has been said "A House divided against itself cannot stand. " The goal of this program is to heal the split in your mind so you can live as the divine intended you to live.
I know you are probably eager to get to the exercises, but this book would not be complete if I did not go on to explain just a little about how the brain is involved; the brain and the subconscious mind are intertwined. They create cycles of either happiness or despair in our lives. After that we will start getting into the more esoteric aspects of this book.

CHAPTER 3: THE CHAIN REACTION

The subconscious and the brain are spokes in the same wheel. Often I find that books of this genre gloss over brain function and stick to the thought aspect alone without shedding light as to HOW the subconscious and brain work together. We have established that your subconscious mind creates the template for the good or bad behavior and habits you have. The brain compels you into action or inaction. First there is thought or event and then there is action and then the loop begins. If you focus enough on something with enough emotion, you will eventually resonate with it and you attract those events to you or rather, you will be attracted to those events. Some call it the "Law of Attraction", but I am not convinced such a law exists in the way it is usually described.

In this chapter I will give you some insight as to how the brain and the subconscious work and how they can both be reprogrammed and re-wired to get you in a state that will work for you much faster and with tangible results. This chapter will give you the structure and knowledge needed to proceed on to the Switchwords and the Meridian Tapping.

I am now going to cover two concepts that are vital for understanding how the brain works as it pertains to your behaviors and habits. I do not claim to give an exhaustive explanation, but one that will give you a good idea of what is going on in the brain when you try to change your habits and thoughts so you can get to where you want to go in life.

Hebb's Law - Neurons that fire together, wire together

When we want to change our thought patterns or habits we must engage our subconscious mind and in turn, our brains to make neuronal changes so that the new thoughts and habits can take effect. You want to exchange bad habits for good ones. It is not enough to think positive or take action only once, it must be done repeatedly. The brain is an association machine and it learns through repetition. In Hebbs law it states "Cells that fire together, wire together" I am sure you may have heard this before. That is Hebbs Law. When a person is addicted to either negative thought patterns or a substance the associations in the brain get stronger. It is not unlike working out a muscle. If you work out regularly the muscle gets bigger and stronger, you will notice that the muscle no longer gets sore because it got used to it. The same phenomenon is happening when you consistently engage in negative thinking or in bad habits. The neurons that are firing as you engage in negativity simply start firing more and in unison which causes them to make stronger connections, thus making it VERY hard to break . This causes your subconscious mind to get used to it. The good news is, if you use the techniques in this book, you will start clearing the negative associations you have.

Focusing on what you want in addition to using these techniques will start weakening the negative neuronal connections and start creating and strengthening positive ones. As I said in the previous chapters, your subconscious mind and brain are simply trying to protect you from being in situations that it thinks will inflict damage, although in the process, they inflict even more damage. If you introduce negative thoughts and behaviors regularly, it will entrench in your mind. I know this may sound rather simplistic, but this is what is happening. Repetition leads to cells firing together which causes them to wire together. I am repeating myself for a reason :).

The Quantum Zeno Effect

A common phrase used in self help literature is "energy flows where attention goes". This has become a cliché amongst the self help and law of attraction communities and has been used ad naseum. However, it is true and there is REAL scientific evidence to prove it. I emphasize real because often you will find many books of this genre loaded with scientific claims that have not really been truly observed. The Quantum Zeno Effect is different; I stumbled upon this scientific evidence after using a Switchword that I will get into later. Like many people, I loved the quote "energy flows where attention goes" but I wanted to know more about how attention related to energy. When I stumbled upon the Quantum Zeno effect, I realized I found the answer I was looking for. While I was considering this chapter on Quantum Zeno Effect, I was having difficulty breaking it down in a way that it would be understandable. Despite my initial difficulties, I knew intuitively that I should include it here and had to make it work.

The reason I added this section to the book is because The Quantum Zeno Effect gives insight into why all this works so well. It will also shed light on the reason we often get trapped in negative, self sabotaging patterns. Although Hebbs Law explains how, with repetition, something becomes linked in the brain; Quantum Zeno Effect explains why this happens.

Quantum Zeno Effect is all about focused attention. It has been proven that when you focus on something, your brains chemistry is altered. The Quantum Zeno Effect states that when you focus your attention on an experience or thought, the act of focusing maintains the brain state that arises in association with that experience. If you focus attention on a given experience, the circuitry in the brain that is associated with that experience remains in a very stable state. When this stability is sustained, Hebbs law kicks in and the neurons associated with this thought and experience will start creating pathways in the brain and new behaviors and or reactions will start taking shape. As you know, in order to change anything, there must be sufficient attention placed on the object or experience you desire in order for you to experience it. The implications of this effect is huge. You can literally change your brain with focused attention. The subconscious mind is fed by this and is feeding these two concepts.

Let me illustrate how this works and why just using mental tricks like affirmations won't remedy the problems you may have in your life.

The Chain reaction: Let's use a hypothetical person by the name of George. He had a fairly rough childhood and was told he wouldn't amount to anything in life. Because of his early childhood, George suffers from worthiness issues which have caused him to sabotage his work and personal life when he became an adult. Let's see how the subconscious, Hebbs Law and The Quantum Zeno effect work together to create situations in his life that keep him stuck in a frame of mind of unworthiness. This illustration is a rough example of how it works and is not meant to illustrate the whole process.

Conscious Mind. Step 1: He is told by an important figure in his life that he is unworthy and will not amount to anything. This probably happened often. The thought of being unworthy is too painful for him to process or understand at first, so it gets buried.

Subconscious Mind. Step 2: As I stated earlier, feelings buried alive, will never die. These thoughts incubate in the subconscious mind, but may not be causing any negative effects in his life, at least not yet. He hasn't been exposed to life yet so for now the trauma may not poison him.

Conscious Mind. Step 3: An event occurs in his life that reinforces what is being harbored in his subconscious mind. He goes through a breakup and it hurts him deeply.

Subconscious Mind. Step 4: The subconscious mind is now given an additional event to store under the "unworthy file". But now George is starting to think that he may very well be unworthy.

Conscious Mind. Step 5: Suddenly whenever something goes wrong, he immediately links this to being unworthy and his thoughts of unworthiness grow. He just can't catch a break.

Subconscious Mind. Step 6: The subconscious mind is now alerted that he is experiencing pain and files away all these associations and is now on the look out to keep him safely in his unworthiness.

Quantum Zeno Effect. Step 7: He starts continually entertaining thoughts of how unworthy he is and he uses all his unfortunate events as proof, suddenly the Quantum Zeno effect kicks in and his attention has now acutely focused on this. His brain circuitry is being engaged.

Hebbs Law. (Action Step) Step 8: The thoughts have now become so numerous that neurons start firing together, creating a pathway in his brain that will be reinforced every time he engages in this negative chain of thought.

Life event Step 9: It's at this point that his subconscious mind will push thoughts of unworthiness out into the world and those thoughts will make him act a certain way and will attract circumstances that will cause him, through Hebbs Law to sabotage himself . These self sabotaging sprees cause more events to occur that go through this process and it goes on and on in a seemingly endless loop. The acts of self sabotage and the events that ensue compound on themselves and get so intense that the Quantum Zeno effect is causing Hebb's Law to be engaged pretty much 24 hours a day. It will also start bubbling over into his sleep and cause nightmares. The Quantum Zeno Effect and Hebbs law do not stop when you are asleep. In fact they are very powerful in your sleeping state. That is why it is imperative to go to bed engaging in the techniques in this book.

In the above scenario, affirmations alone cannot help George because this is now beyond just mere words, his unworthiness has become his entire energy field so to speak. He has become a lightning rod for negative circumstances. He needs more than words at this point; he needs more than just visualization. He needs to address every aspect of this issue. It's a fact that negative energy is stored in other areas of the body, not just the mind. It's for this reason I have incorporated Meridian tapping in this book. The Meridian Tapping allows for blocks in your body's energy to be released which helps the mind as well. The switchwords help you free your mind and focus your attention (Quantum Zeno Effect) which in turn allows you to clear your mind and body even further by communicating directly with the subconscious mind with practically no resistance. Meridian tapping takes a few of the roadblocks away so the switchwords can work more powerfully. When this happens, an endless loop of positivity is created and the regular tapping and switchword use creates an atmosphere of powerful and beneficial results. Positive and synchronistic events will show up and you will be compelled to act because your brain is now wired to take action (Hebbs law) , positive action that is.

As promised, this was going to be short chapter; I just wanted to give you an idea of what is going in the brain when these things occur. It is by far not comprehensive, we could go on about neurotransmitters and the like, but for our purposes, this will suffice.

Ok now we are going to jump into what Meridian tapping and switchwords are. We are almost there, change is coming. Bear with me; it will be well worth your time.

Chapter 4: The Energy System / Getting Clear

We are only 3 more chapters away from getting to the actual techniques. I am covering quite a bit of information here. It can seem overwhelming at first but once we get to the exercises and start practicing all this, it will become easy. I have done my best to be as concise as possible , I left out many hundreds of pages worth of material that are not, in my estimation, useful for the person who wants to make radical changes in their lives.

Before we go into the details of Meridian tapping I want to discuss our energy system and the concept of getting clear. In the self help field there are thousands of techniques on clearing negative beliefs, some are complex and expect you to do things that are seemingly impossible and run counter to your daily life. For starters, what we need to do is not just think positively in order to get clear, we have to really clear the negative energy itself, not just bury it in positive words. We need to upend the negative structure itself and not just paint it pretty colors. It's for this reason I incorporated Meridian tapping into this book. Meridian tapping engages the negative thoughts so they become conscious and then it exposes them and either brings relief right away or allows you to explore further. For persistent negative thinking it may take longer, but with consistency you can defeat almost any negative thought. Meridian tapping is a tool that will help you do that. Switchwords will enhance this even further and can also work on its own.

Meridian tapping is more commonly known as E.F.T or Emotional freedom technique. Meridian tapping and Switchwords alone have worked well for me. It was only when I combined them that I realized how powerful they really are. Meridian tapping is miraculously simple for such a powerful technique. Sometimes it's the simple solutions that are most effective. In this case, less really is more. You don't need to meditate for hours on end to get results, that is, unless you like to meditate for hours. From my experience, most people I speak to do not have the time nor the will to sit like a monk. The world is moving too fast for that and we need effective tools to adapt ourselves to this fast-paced environment.

We have been talking a lot about energy and attention and how they work together in either making our lives pure joy or making it pure hell. In order for you to truly understand how Meridian tapping works I will need to describe the various levels and types of energy that exists within the Mind-Body. By being armed with this knowledge you will be able to get a better picture of what is going on when you use the exercises in this book. In this chapter we will be covering Chakra energies, Kundalini, Prana (subtle energy), Nadis or energy channels, and of course Meridian points. These energies are the fuel behind The Conscious mind - Subconscious mind - Quantum Zeno Effect - Hebbs Law continuum. In short, it's your life energy , the subconscious mind feeds and is fed by this energy. It's an energetic loop.

Since it is the energy system we are primarily concerned with in this chapter, I am going to dedicate some time on this in order to make it clear. It is not exhaustive but will suffice for the purposes of this book. It is important for understanding Meridian points.

I would like to note that not every negative thing in your life is due to a catastrophic energy imbalance or an overactive subconscious mind; sometimes it is simply a matter of correcting a slight imbalance. Although you may experience quite dramatic negativity in your life, it could very well be a matter of a slight energy imbalance and nothing more. Do not be surprised if you experience quick relief from something you think may be too large for you to handle. Again, for legal purposes I can't make any guarantees, all I can tell you is that if you give this book an honest attempt, I feel you will gain a lot from it. You don't have to believe any of this in order for it to work, that's the beauty of these techniques.

The Energy System:

Chakras:

Chakras have gained much attention over the years; you will find countless yoga instructors using chakra meditation during yoga sessions. There are countless books on the chakra system, some quite scholarly and some that seem a bit "far out". For our purposes I am going to try to bridge the gap between the dry scholarly work and the "far out" ideas involving the chakras.

The word Chakra comes from the Sanskrit word cakram which means wheel. In Hindu art they are often depicted as flowers with a set number of petals. These petals are interconnected in such a way that they appear as spokes in a wheel, they are visualized as whirling wheels of energy situated along the spine in what is called the "Subtle Body". The subtle body is in essence an energetic double of ourselves. This double is not fully outside of us, but intertwined with our physical body. Due to this intertwining with the body, energy flowing through the subtle body affects everything in the physical body. These energy centers are the main avenue for the reception and transmission of energy both physically and spiritually.

The whole concept of the Chakra system has been gleaned from ancient Hindu texts. Some of these texts may be the oldest text in existence. There are 7 chakra centers in our bodies, some traditions say that we have more, but for our purposes we will deal with the more common view that we have 7 chakras.
In the illustration below you will see where the various chakras are. I will give a description of each one here.

© M.Gove - Fotolia.com

The Root Chakra

The first Chakra or Root Chakra called Mūlādhāra in Sanskrit is at the base of the spine and forms the foundation for our physical well being. It Is found at the level of where the ovaries in a woman and prostate in a man would be. This Chakra is very much connected to the body and physical activities. When you engage the root chakra you are firmly rooting yourself to the physical world. Since this is the root chakra, the energy life force or Kundalini is coiled at the bottom of it, waiting to move up the chakras as we develop our spirituality. Although it is predominantly earth centered, it is very powerful. This Chakra must be harmonized if we are going to live in this world. Often imbalances at the root chakra leads to several physical ailments such as sexual dysfunction and reproductive issues, blood and circulatory problems which can be quite severe, constipation amongst other issues. When we harmonize this chakra, we are able to feel safe and secure in this world. I am working on a text right now that will get into the specific switchwords for each Chakra as well as information about the different crystals that are associated with each chakra. If you would like to be notified when this text will be available, please join our mailing list at http://www.switchwordmiracles.com

The Sacral Chakra

The second chakra or Sacral Chakra called Svādhiṣṭhāna in Sanskrit . It is situated right at the last bone of the Spine or above the sex organs. This Chakra deals with our emotions and our sexuality. When this chakra is harmonized it can help us make emotional connections. This chakra holds our desires and feelings at its core. Imbalances may appear as hormonal imbalances, muscular tension, and depression amongst other things.

The Solar Plexus Chakra

The third chakra or Solar Plexus Chakra called Maṇipūra in Sanskrit. It is situated in the navel area, approximately between the rib cage and your belly button. This chakra is often the location the body double leaves when you experience an out of body experience. This is a very important and sensitive chakra. Because it is located at the core of the body, it is often known as the "power" chakra. Imbalances in this chakra can include all intestinal ailments, as well as liver, kidneys, spleen. It is also associated with diabetes and arthritis amongst other things. When this chakra is aligned it can be a great source of energy for us. This is no surprise, science has proven that our stomach is essentially our second brain and has more neurons than our spinal column does. When this Chakra is balanced it can change everything for us. I feel most of us could use aligning in this chakra.

The Heart Chakra

The fourth chakra or Heart Chakra called Anāhata in Sanskrit. It is situated in the heart area itself. This Chakra is extremely important because it is an energy converter. It takes the very high vibration energy from the top 3 chakras and converts it so the lower 3 can use the energy. If the heart chakra does not convert this energy this could translate into dramatic hardships for the person. The obvious imbalance of this chakra is heart disease and pulmonary issues. Since it is the converter of energy, it also has the ability to integrate different vibrational patterns so they remain in harmony. It allows us to integrate the body-mind continuum and keeps the different parts of your being in harmony. Often we may find ourselves in extreme emotional states; a harmonized heart center will help balance the extremes out and leaves peace in its wake.

The Throat Chakra

The fifth chakra or Throat Chakra called Viśuddha in Sanskrit. It is situated in the throat area itself. This chakra is the center of communication, not only for our various interactions with the outside world but also communication with ourselves. It helps us translate our feelings that stir in our minds into words. Poets, writers and linguists often have very strong Throat Chakra energy. An imbalanced Throat Chakra can make you more susceptible to colds and flus, vocal and communication problems, thyroid disorders amongst other things. Often people, who can't speak up for themselves or feel stifled, have imbalances in the throat chakra. When we say the switchwords (Next chapter) out loud they automatically help this chakra since the sound is originating from the throat and mouth.

The Third Eye Chakra or Brow Chakra

The sixth chakra or Brow Chakra called Ājñā in Sanskrit. It is situated right between the eyes. Our 3rd eyes exist in this area. The third eye gives us the power to see things with "different eyes". It helps to see things as they really are and not just based on our senses. It is the seat of our intuition. When we use our intuition we are engaging the third eye. This is another location where the astral body can leave the body during out of body experiences. A developed third eye is a step closer to divine bliss, a state where the things of the world will no longer bother you or affect you.

An imbalance in the Third eye chakra causes memory and cognitive issues, migraine headaches, insomnia, neuropathic pain, high blood pressure, and problems with the sinuses amongst other things. It also causes us to lose touch with our spirituality when we have a third eye imbalance. This is a very important chakra that must be aligned.

The Crown Chakra

The seventh chakra or Crown Chakra called Sahasrāra in Sanskrit. It is situated right at the top of the head. This chakra serves as your spiritual gateway. It is also the location where life/divine energy enters into the chakra system and your body. It is no coincidence that in almost every religion, gods, prophets and holy people all had a light shine from the tops of their heads in the form of halos. That shine is from a developed Crown Chakra. An imbalance in the Crown Chakra can cause self centeredness, but a special form of self centeredness called Spiritual narcissism. Spiritual narcissism develops when a person has such a strong sense of spirituality that instead of channeling that for the benefit of others it translates into feelings of superiority. This is very pervasive in the self help community. An imbalance at this chakra can also lead to some astounding delusions. When this chakra is developed we experience deep understanding, spiritual connection and bliss. This level has no concern for duality. It has transcended both time and space.

Kundalini and Prana

The energy that flows through the chakras is called Kundalini. Kundalini can also be referred to as Shakti. The word Kundalini means "Coiled", it is called this because it is visualized in the form of a snake coiled up at the base of the spine or root chakra.

When we start engaging the chakras, this energy slowly unravels and works its way up the body. Since this energy is mostly feminine in nature, another name used for it is Shakti, Shakti is the embodiment of feminine energy in the universe. Shakti and Kundalini can be used interchangeably.

Now Prana is slightly different but it is interrelated. Prana is defined in Sanskrit as "life force". This, in its simplest form can best be described as the "Elan Vital", vital life force. It is because of Prana that we are able to physically function, the subconscious regulates this as well. This energy travels throughout a network of pathways in our bodies called Nadis or Meridians. Prana makes sure that all our bodily functions are working. It's a tad difficult to describe this energy because the force itself is intangible and spiritual. These energies are responsible for all of our psychophysical needs.

In order to explain both Prana and Kundalini let us try to relate the two. Prana as I mentioned is responsible for much of our psychophysical needs. In essence, kundalini is almost identical to Prana; however, Kundalini has a far wider reach than Prana. Tapping into Kundalini can lead us to very high states of being. Pranic energy work is simply a stepping stone to Kundalini work. This is important to know because in the west, many people practice Kundalini yoga thinking they are doing a good thing but in fact they are causing much more damage to themselves. If they have Pranic blocks, awakening Kundalini can be quite a negative experience. It is like trying to force a baby to run before it can walk. The baby risks serious injury. Switchwords and Meridian tapping together help release the blocks in Prana which then allows us to work on our Chakras, in fact, the Chakras will immediately self regulate once the blockage is gone. Which really means the subconscious is finally working in your favor. It is for this reason you will find that during the exercises; I will do an initial tapping sequence to get clear. Getting clear is essential in order to release pranic blocks. You must be clear before you get into the deeper work. It's a step I deem to be nonnegotiable. The clearing has to be done to make it to the next stage. The next section will illustrate why clearing is so important.

Nadis and Meridian points.

Nadi in Sanskrit means river or channel; there are many Nadi points in the body. These points are located on the physical body as well as the subtle body. They are used to transport energetic substances in and out of our bodies, both subtle and physical. More specifically, in Hindu texts they are channels for the life force or Prana. In Chinese acupuncture, nadis are referred to as meridian points. Our quality of life depends on the ease of which energy flows throughout these points. In order to remain healthy in both mind and body, the nadis/meridian points must be unblocked. If they are blocked, they can cause untold misery in your life both physically and mentally. Since these points are throughout the body any blockage in any of them inevitably causes physical ailments as well. Remember, the subconscious causes these blocks from unresolved issues. The Nadis that are in the subtle body are channels for our many thoughts and feelings both positive and negative. When the subtle energy is blocked, we grow complacent with life. We isolate from others and can often fall into deep depression. These blocks also cause us to make decisions that are not so wise.

The chakras as I mentioned earlier in the chapter play a very important role in how our energy is regulated. Since the Nadis are conduits of energy, they are very important for the energy flows in and out of our chakras and elsewhere in the body. Since these Nadis and Meridian points are vast in number, I have chosen a few to work with. When we use Switchwords and Meridian tapping together we can unblock any blockages you may have. You are of course welcome to use each one separately. You will know which one to focus on after you go through this book. Once we clear out the main energetic arteries we can let the full energetic potential of our lives express itself and flow. These energies are so powerful, often; once they are cleared, it immediately reprograms and overrides the subconscious mind. It can literally undo years of trauma. This clearing will also allow you to clearly work towards your goals. The first step is to clear those energy pathways.

The next chapter I will go into Meridian tapping specifically and how it is done and some background. Then in the final section of part 1 we will delve into why switchwords are so vital for the clearing and manifestation processes to occur. In part 2, you will start your journey to a new and more mindful life.

CHAPTER 5:MERIDIAN TAPPING

Perhaps you have heard about EFT, it has been very popular for many years amongst the energy healing crowd. EFT is an acronym for Emotional Freedom Technique and as the name implies, it is a method of freeing yourself from negative emotional states. It alone is highly effective and the EFT methods are evolving every day and becoming even more effective. People have found relief and even cures for chronic painful conditions. As I mentioned in the chapter about the subconscious mind, often when emotions are buried alive it can cause psychosomatic illness. EFT is one of the most effective remedies for such illnesses.

EFT aka Meridian Tapping is a form of psychological acupressure that uses the traditional ancient Chinese acupuncture points that correspond to the meridians of the body. Instead of using needles, however, you would use your fingers to gently tap on the various meridian points. As you tap you will also express the issue you are having, either out loud or in your mind. The combination of verbalization and tapping create a very powerful synergy. And it is even more powerful when using switchwords and tapping. We will get into that in part 2.

EFT evolved over time from a technique called "Thought field therapy." T.F.T also includes tapping meridian points but was a bit more complex in its approach. Gary Craig, a performance coach from California eventually simplified the approach and called it EFT. He chose a set of meridian points to focus on and developed the technique around them. The wonderful thing about Meridian tapping is that it doesn't take a long time to implement. In less than 2 minutes you can go through an entire cycle of meridian points. For the purposes of this book, I am going to use some Gary Craig's choice of Meridian points since they are the least complicated and are easily accessible. As I mentioned earlier, Meridian tapping is a very powerful approach to releasing emotional blocks and various physical conditions that cause pain. When you tap the meridian points it affects your entire energy system and that is why it often yields such dramatic results. It is also very powerful against addictions, depression, phobias. It can also be used to imprint positive goals on to your subconscious mind. In short, it is a technique that can transform your life. Below is a chart of the Meridian points we will be using.

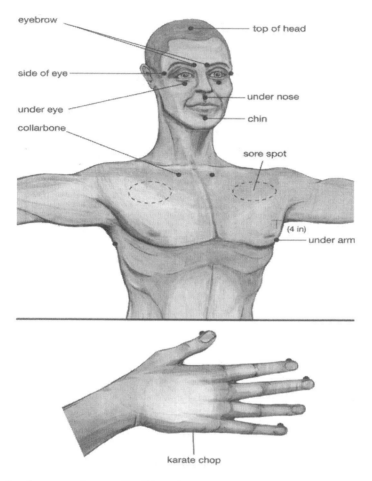

eyebrow
top of head
side of eye
under nose
under eye
chin
collarbone
sore spot
(4 in)
under arm

karate chop

In the next chapter I will go into switchwords, the core of this book and the words that will change everything for you.

CHAPTER 6: SWITCHWORDS

We are now entering a very exciting part of this book, I will be going into some detail about Switchwords and how they can change your life. I will provide a comprehensive list of all the main Switchwords also known as "universal" and "Master" Switchwords at the end of the chapter.

I stumbled upon Switchwords by "accident". I was going through a breakup and I have to say, it was a really dark moment for me. It was my fault, I had negative emotional habits that caused me to become overly sensitive which in turn caused me to stagnant in life and not take chances. Unfortunately, there are emotional consequences to being in that state. Consequences that inevitably led to losing a woman I loved so much. In fact, she is "the girl that got away". This was a bitterly painful time.

I forgot what exact search term I was using on Google, but somehow I was guided to Switchwords. I have read hundreds if not thousands of books in the self help and spiritual genres and thought I had pretty much seen it all. Nothing new and innovative was coming out and despite having a brain full of transformative tools; I felt I was missing a piece of the puzzle. I was very frustrated because I wasn't able to get the results I wanted from my subconscious mind and it was certainly not for the lack of trying. Something was missing and I needed a boost and I needed it fast. It was at that low point when Switchwords appeared. I have never heard of them before and doing a search I could see that it wasn't showing up like the other methods that saturate the internet with millions of search results. Put in "law of attraction" (with the quotation marks to focus the search results) and you get 15,200,000, that is over fifteen million results, It's everywhere. Now put in "Switchwords" and you get 21,400, that is slightly over twenty one thousand results. That is a very low number in terms of search results. I felt that I was on to something, something that few people know about. I researched them further and I am glad I did. I am a different person today because of them and now I am bringing them to you, so you too can be transformed.

What are Switchwords and how were they discovered?

Switchwords were created or shall I say discovered by James T. Mangan. In his book "The Secret of Perfect Living" he states that the subconscious mind has several "switches" that when flipped, can result in certain outcomes. Shunyam Nirav has also contributed greatly to the understanding of Switchwords. He is the author of "Switchwords Easily Give to You Whatever You Want in Life". These switches are certain words or a combination of words.. In many ways they are one-word affirmations or a string of one word affirmations, unlike sentences, or affirmations like "I am wonderful just as I am " they don't make sense in the conventional sense of the word. The conventional affirmations contain statements that your subconscious does not believe is true (that's why they generally do not work as I stated earlier in this book). Switchwords , however, bypass the "interpretive" aspect of your mind and engage the subconscious mind directly thus making the result automatic. This is vital because if your communications with the subconscious mind are drawn out like affirmations, you are giving the subconscious mind the opportunity to cancel those affirmation and dig in, thus making change harder.

With Switchwords it is a switch, there is no opportunity for the subconscious mind to block or interpret it. It simply switches the state on. Sometimes it requires a few repetitions, but it works. I swear by it. If you do research you won't find many people saying negative things about them. You may ask, 'If Switchwords are so powerful, why combine them with EFT?" In reality you don't have to, but I found it adds an additional kick to the results. You can use both modalities separately if you like. I find that Switchwords are the more powerful of the two modalities. They are enhanced when used in conjunction with EFT. It's for this reason I named this book "Switchword miracles" Instead of "A novel approach to EFT". Switchwords are the core modality.

Some have asked me 'If Switchwords are so effective, why haven't I heard of them?" I asked the same question. I have come to realize they are not as popular because they simply aren't attractive and flashy like the other kinds of modalities. They can't be packaged with flowery language and you can't really create countless elaborate exercises. They are simple and paired down and that is not what this industry is looking for. I know that is a harsh indictment of the industry but if you look at what is out there, they are made appealing to the senses and flashy. That doesn't mean they are effective. I feel the industry has steered away from quality and focused more on quantity and packaging. It has become very commercial. I think Self-help should be exactly that, SELF HELP and in saying that, I believe results are more important than packaging. Don't you agree?

Sorry for the diversion, now back to the origin and elaboration of Switchwords. James Mangan identified approximately 100 Switchwords that are extremely effective when used with a specific goal in mind. Others have added to the list as well. The beauty of using Switchwords is that you don't need to believe it will work in order for it to. It's like gravity, you can say it doesn't exist until you are blue in the face but it will work on you regardless of whether you believe in it or not. This is another reason why Switchwords are more effective than traditional affirmations. There is no belief involved. I know I am sounding like a broken record here but it is very important to keep this in mind. With conventional affirmation you are told to believe the affirmation is true. I don't know about you, but it was VERY hard for me to believe that " I am perfect as I am and I have unlimited money in the bank". As I mentioned earlier, the subconscious will kick that idea out and may even entrench the opposite of that affirmation even deeper. In this way, conventional affirmations can be dangerous. It may make your current situation worse because the subconscious mind wants to entrench it deeper after being exposed to the conventional affirmation that it knows to be false.

It is no wonder why so many people seem to get worse after using the Law of Attraction in the conventional way. They are fighting an entrenched force the wrong way... in this case, less is more my friend.

In essence, Switchwords capture the core and energy of a desired result or experience. There is no right or wrong way to use them, you can sing them, declare them, chant them or say them in the quiet of your own mind. Say them once or thousands of times a day, whatever way you feel will create results for you. Just remember that more is not always better. Sometimes just mentioning them once a day will work just fine. No matter how you use them, they work and you really can't go wrong.

Here are a few examples of how you can use Switchwords:

Let's say you want to get in the mood to write you can simply say the Switchword "GIGGLE" either once or several times and you will notice that you will start getting in the mood to write. Lets say you lost something, you can use the Switchword " REACH" and it will guide you in the right direction. REACH can also be used to retrieve a memory or "reach" for a new idea or solution to a problem.

I often use the Switchwords " UP" and "MOVE" when I need extra energy and within a few minutes that energy comes to me. In fact I use the Switchwords ," UP-MOVE- HALFWAY" when I run and it really helps right away. I wouldn't be able to run like I do without saying those 3 words. I also say UP-MOVE when I wake up. It works.

I will now provide you with a comprehensive list of Switchwords and their respective uses. The list below contains "Universal or Master Switchwords" that James mentions in his book. I will also go into how you can create your own Switchwords. Many of the Switchwords can be used interchangeably so you may find one word feels better to use than another for your particular situation. You will also notice that many Switchwords can be used in several different situations.

Universal / Master Switchwords and how they can help you:

ACT: If you would like to become a good speaker.
ADD: This is to increase what you have, no matter what it is.
ADJUST: This is a great one to create balance in your life. It will also help you handle uncomfortable or unpleasant conditions.
ALONE: This will help you nurture or heal yourself or another. This will help you increase focus on yourself but not in a self absorbed way but in terms of nurturing and healing yourself.
AROUND: This will help you gain or improve your perspective.
ATTENTION: This will help you do detailed work and avoid carelessness. This will apply to other areas of your life as well, not only work.
BE: This is a powerful one, this will help you to achieve peace and good health. It will help you have good form; dispel loneliness; increase your skill in sports. It also has the added benefit of helping you brush off ridicule from others.
BETWEEN: This one is often used to develop intuition and psychic abilities. It works.
BLUFF: This one is good to get rid of nervousness or fear as well as increase your imagination. It is especially good to use when you want to create pleasant dreams.
BOW: This helps reduce any arrogant tendencies you may have.

BRING: This is a manifestation Switchword, it helps you unite with your goal, helps you finish what you started.

BUBBLE: This Switchword is really good at helping you expand your perceived limits, it is also good for creating a mood of excitement and energy.

CANCEL: Use this Switchword to eliminate negative thoughts and conditions. It helps eliminate debt, poverty and other unwanted conditions. Which in turn will dispel worry. I use this one when I feel insecure about something.

CANCER: To clarify, this does not mean cancer the disease but rather the zodiac sign. This Switchword is used to calm emotional distress and to soften outlook.

CARE: This one is used to help you retain or memorize anything you need to remember or retain. You can say it before you read something so as to remember it.

CHANGE: This helps get rid of emotional and physical pain. It also helps get something out of the eye.

CHARLTON HESTON: I admit, I feel silly saying this one sometimes but it is good to keep you mindful about your posture. Helps you stand straight and tall. You can use someone elses names who stands straight or tall with confidence.

CHARM: This will help you manifest your heart's desire.

CHLORINE: This will help you mingle and share yourself with others. Helps you make a difference; blend in and become one with.

CHUCKLE: This one helps you turn on personality.

CIRCULATE: This helps you end loneliness and helps you feel at ease so you can mingle with people. CLASSIC: Use this one to appear cultured and suave .

CLEAR: This one will help you dispel anger and resentment you may towards yourself or others.

CLIMB: This will help you enhance your view point, rise above it all.

CONCEDE: This helps to reconcile and end arguments between people. You can use it if you want to be at peace with someone.

CONFESS: This ends aggression very well.

CONSIDER: This helps you become more handy . use it before fixing your car or putting together a piece of future etc.

CONTINUE: This helps create or increase endurance for both physical and mental tasks.

COPY: this helps you have good taste and also increases fertility.

COUNT: This will help you make money and help you reduce or stop smoking

COVER: reduce nervousness; subdue inner excitement

CRISP: This is a great one to dispel fatigue, feel refreshed, revitalizes. It also helps brighten your mood. CROWD: This helps reduce or eliminate disobedience in children, pets or subordinates ant work.

CRYSTAL: This is a powerful Switchword that will help you clarify any situation or things. It helps you look to the future; both mentally and through clairvoyance. This can help you access Universal Knowledge. I use this one to clarify intentions when I feel blocked.

CURVE: This helps to create beauty; make something beautiful. This is good to enhance creativity.

CUT: This will help you achieve moderation in all your actions. It can also help you make proactive decisions regarding toxic relationships. Essentially giving you the strength to sever ties with a toxic person if you have to.

CUTE: This will help you think; discern; be sharp-witted and be clever.

DEDICATE: This will help you to stop clinging to either a person or a situation.

DIVINE: This one will help you work miracles or accomplish extraordinary things, it increases personal ability.

DIVINE LIGHT: This will help you focus on positivity, multiply the intensity of any thought; increase spiritual enlightenment.

DIVINE ORDER: This will help you with any organizing or cleaning you need to do. It helps you be more efficient making sure things are in optimal order. I use this when I feel disorganized with my thoughts or do not know where to start something. It helps bring order.

DO: eliminate procrastination in its tracks with this one.

DONE: This is a great one against procrastination as well . It helps you meet a deadline or keep a resolution. It's great for building willpower.

DOWN: This helps you become more humble. People don't like braggarts , this will help eliminate that trait in you if bragging is a problem for you.

DUCK: This helps dispel sensitivity about looks or capabilities. Helps you shrug off criticism.

ELATE: This helps transform a setback into a positive uplifting event.

FIFTY THREE (53): This helps you take primary responsibility over something.

FIGHT: This helps you win a competitive game and intensify your efforts and intentions.

FIND: This helps you build a fortune and can be used with Switchword "COUNT".

FOR: This will help you promote anything.

FOREVER: This will help you keep a secret.

FORGIVE: This will help you cool your anger and end desire for revenge . This also helps dispel remorse. FULL: This helps you achieve optimum levels to help you go beyond and expand your capacity in any endeavor.

GIGGLE: This will get you in the mood for writing. It will also help you enjoy the task at hand.

GIVE: To sell something and to help others.

GO: This will help you end laziness. Helps you begin and progress in anything. I use it when I feel like I don't want to start something right away. I say GO and I get motivated.

GUARD: This helps protect you from bodily hard, spirit or your property. it helps to preserve your personal safety.

HALFWAY: This helps make a long distance seem short. This is one of 3 Switchwords I use to make my long runs easier. It also helps me better handle projects that require long tedious work.

HELP: This helps eliminate indecision or uncertainty and increases focus.

HO: Saying this one helps you relax and reduce tension.

HOLD: This helps to build character.

HOLE: This will help create attractiveness and sex appeal in yourself.

HORSE: This will help you be solid, strong and gain personal power .

HORSESHOE: This will help you remain steadfast and strengthen the soul during times of challenge. It will help you safely move rapidly ahead and remain sturdy throughout.

JACK LALANNE: this will help you be enthusiastic (or you use someone you know who is an enthusiast about something)

JUDGE: This will help you love reading and increase your comprehension of what you read. I use this all the time when I read.

LEARN: act and be youthful; rejuvenate your mind and soul.

LIGHT: This will help you be inspired, lighten the load or mood. It's a great stress reducer.

LIMIT: set parameters, regain control. This will help keep others from taking advantage of you.

LISTEN: This will help you predict the future. This is also very powerful when you want to get in touch with nature and yourself.

LOVE: This will help generate, radiate and experience love of all types.

MAGNANIMITY: This will help you eliminate pettiness and increase generosity.

MASK: Protect and shield from harm .

MONA LISA: This will help bring a smile to your face and dispel hatred and envy. (Or you can use someone who represents a smile to you)

MOVE: This is great to increase energy and eliminate tiredness. It is one of the 3 words I use every time I run, without fail.

NEXT: This will help you finish lots of meticulous work and be able to endure more.

NOW: This ends procrastination. It also helps you to act on good impulses.

OFF: This one is used to quit an unwanted habit AND it helps you go to sleep. This Switchword does help me sleep. If I wake up in the middle of the night, I can rely on "OFF" to help me get back to sleep quickly. I love it.

OFFER: This will help dispel greed.

OIL: This will help external and internal friction. Smooth and release tensions and resistance.

ON: This is a very powerful Switchword to help you get new ideas; obtain transportation; nourish your ambition.

OPEN: This will he help free you from inhibitions. It will increase tolerance and understanding. it can free the mind and allow feeling and ideas to flow easily.

OVER: This will help end frustration.

PERSONAL: This will help you be a success. It will help you publish a successful newspaper or a newsletter or book for that matter.

PHASE: This will help you set goals. Set a routine or pattern and improve your situation.

POINT: This will improve eyesight and focus. It will help you find direction and make a clear decision. POSTPONE: This helps you to let things go.

PRAISE: This will help you be beautiful or handsome and will help you to stop being overly critical with yourself.

PUT: This will help you build and expand. You can use this for any endeavor you want to build or expand. QUIET: This will help quiet the ego. If you feel you must get the last word in, say QUIET and you will notice how that urge will subside. I used this the other day and I was able to just let it all go and let the other person have their moment.

REACH: This is great to locate misplaced objects and reach solutions for problems. It will help you repair things. It will help you recall forgotten ideas and information in your mind or memory like names, numbers etc. I used this twice and it worked very well. I am not one to lose my keys, in fact, I NEVER DO. When I did, I used this Switchword and I found it very quickly and in the most unlikely place. The fridge. (I have no idea how they got in there).

REJOICE: When you encounter someone who is more successful in something that you want success in, it is easy to feel jealous. This Switchword will help dispel jealousy.

RESCIND: This will help you undo; restart; cancel; redo; something. Some other teachers of Switchwords recommend that this switchword should Always be used with the Switchwords;BETWEEN, CRYSTAL and LISTEN in order to avoid as they say "possible time loop." I can't say I know exactly what that means, but erring on the side of caution can't hurt.

RESTORE: This will help restore fairness and honesty .

REVERSE: This will help you get rid of grudges or stop a

repetitive pattern in the moment.

RIDICULOUS: This will help you gain a lot of attention.

ROOT: This will help you discover and grow in any area of your life.

SAGE: To help you dispel evil in the mind or your home.

SAVE: This will help you stop drinking alcohol and other unwanted habits. I used this word with POSTPONE to help me when I was drinking a lot.

SCHEME: This is great for those of you who want to advertise, design and create marketing plans or PR for your company or business.

SHOW: This will help you raise your moral standards and help you develop respect for people and yourself. SHUT: When you feel a bit reckless and sad, use this to help you stop looking for trouble.

SOPHISTICATE: This will help you publish a successful magazine or book. It will also help you become a great success .

SPEND: This will help you develop a sense of style.

STRETCH: This will help you prolong a good feeling , event or a sense of well-being you are experiencing. It will also help you grow intellectually, spiritually and physically. By grow I mean become better.

SUFFER: This will help you handle success and prosperity . Often we think that once we are successful that it will be easy. Often times it is not, with great success comes great responsibility. This Switchword will help you handle it. I sure could have used this word 10 years ago.

SWEET: This will help you be soothing and caring for others.

SWING: This will raise your courage and boldness.

SWIVEL: relieve constipation and diarrhea. All I am going to say about this one is that...it works.

TAKE: This will help you become a good leader . This is great for people who find that they need to develop leadership skills quickly.

TAP: This will help you convert; adapt; renovate anything.

THANKS: This will help increase gratitude in your heart and will help release guilt.

TINY: This will help you be polite , kind hearted and courteous. It will also you decrease the importance of something that bothers you.

TOGETHER: This is considered to be THE Master Switchword to help you master any activity. Get things all together. It is also used to become single-minded when you need to be. I will mention this one again in the section on how to create Switchwords for yourself. It's the most powerful Switchword in the list.

TOMORROW: This will help you eliminate remorse and sorrow.

UNCLE: dispel un-togetherness and separateness.

UNMASK: This Switchword will help bring things into focus; expose; lay bare before you.

UP: This will help elevate your mood and help you defeat feelings of inferiority.

WAIT: Saying this will create a situation where you will learn a secret.

WASTE: This will help you appear rich and show opulence .

WATCH: This will help you learn a skill or perfect a skill you already have.

WHET: This one will help stimulate, sharpen and refine anything you put your mind upon.

WITH: This will help you be agreeable and compatible with others.

WOMB: This will help you attract and feel cuddled and safe. This will help you reconnect with Divinity and mother nature.

Now I will, for your convenience, create 2 lists of Switchwords. These will contain the specific Switchwords for achieving Wealth, Prosperity and Success and Switchwords for Wellbeing and to acquire ability. I will also add the explanations again so you don't need to scroll back up to the main list. The list I supplied above is more specific and you may choose the ones that are best suited for you. After that, I will go into the various combinations of Switchwords that work well together and then finally, how you can create your own Switchwords. I am including this so when we get to part 2, you will be able to jump right into the exercises... We are almost there.

Switchwords for Wealth , Prosperity and Success:

ACT: If you would like to become a good speaker.

ADD: This is to increase what you have, no matter what it is.

ADJUST: This is a great one to create balance in your life. It will also help you handle uncomfortable or unpleasant conditions.

CANCEL: Use this Switchword to eliminate negative thoughts and conditions. It helps eliminate debt, poverty and other unwanted conditions. Which in turn will dispel worry. I use this one when I feel insecure about something.

CONCEDE: This helps to reconcile and end arguments between people. You can use it if you want to be at peace with someone.

CONFESS: This ends aggression very well.

COUNT: This will help you make money and help you reduce or stop smoking.

CROWD: This helps reduce or eliminate disobedience in children, pets or subordinates ant work.

CUT: This will help you achieve moderation in all your actions. It can also help you make proactive decisions regarding toxic relationships. Essentially giving you the strength to sever ties with a toxic person if you have to.

DO: eliminate procrastination in its tracks with this one.

DONE: This is a great one against procrastination as well . It helps you meet a deadline or keep a resolution. It's great for building willpower .

ELATE: This helps transform a setback into a positive uplifting event.

FIGHT: This helps you win a competitive game and intensify your efforts and intentions.

FIND: This helps you build a fortune and can be used with Switchword "COUNT".

FOR: This will help you promote anything.

GIGGLE: This will get you in the mood for writing. It will also help you enjoy the task at hand.

GIVE: To sell something and to help others.

HALFWAY: This helps make a long distance seem short. This is one of 3 Switchwords I use to make my long runs easier. it also helps me better handle projects that require long tedious work.

MAGNANIMITY: This will help you eliminate pettiness and increase generosity.

NEXT: This will help you finish lots of meticulous work and be able to endure more.

NOW: This ends procrastination. It also helps you to act on good impulses.

ON: This is a very powerful Switchword to help you get new ideas; obtain transportation; nourish your ambition.

PERSONAL: This will help you be a success. It will help you publish a successful newspaper or a newsletter or book for that matter.

PUT: This will help you build and expand. You can use this for any endeavor you want to build or expand.

REACH: This is great to locate misplaced objects and reach solutions for problems. It will help you repair things. It will help you recall forgotten ideas and information in your mind or memory like names, numbers etc. I used this twice and it worked very well. i am not one to lose my keys, in fact, I NEVER DO. When I did, I used this Switchword and I found it very quickly and in the most unlikely place. The fridge. (I have no idea how they got in there).

SCHEME: This is great for those of you who want to advertise, design and create marketing plans or PR for your company or business.

SHOW: This will help you raise your moral standards and help you develop respect for people and yourself.

SOPHISTICATE: This will help you publish a successful magazine or book. It will also help you become a great success .

SPEND: This will help you develop a sense of style.

SUFFER: This will help you handle success and prosperity . Often we think that once we are successful that it will be easy. Often times it is not, with great success comes great responsibility. This Switchword will help you handle it. I sure could have used this word 10 years ago.

TAKE: This will help you become a good leader . This is great for people who find that they need to develop leadership skills quickly.

TOGETHER: This is considered to be THE Master Switchword to help you master any activity. Get things all together. It is also used to become single-minded when you need to be. I will mention this one again in the section on how to create Switchwords for yourself. It's the most powerful Switchword in the list.

WASTE: This will help you appear rich and show opulence.

Switchwords for Wellbeing and to acquire ability:

AROUND: This will help you gain or improve your perspective.

ATTENTION: This will help you do detailed work and avoid carelessness. This will apply to other areas of your life as well, not only work.

BLUFF: This one is good to get rid of nervousness or fear as well as increase your imagination. It is especially good to use when you want to create pleasant dreams.

BOW: This helps reduce any arrogant tendencies you may have.

CARE: This one is used to help you retain or memorize anything you need to remember or retain. You can say it before you read something so as to remember it.

CIRCULATE: This helps you end loneliness and helps you feel at ease so you can mingle with people.

CHUCKLE: This one helps you turn on personality.

CLASSIC: Use this one to appear cultured and suave .

CONSIDER: This helps you become more handy . Use it before fixing your car or putting together a piece of future etc.

CONTINUE: This helps create or increase endurance for both

physical and mental tasks.

COPY: this helps you have good taste and also increases fertility.

COUNT: This will help you make money and help you reduce or stop smoking.

COVER: reduce nervousness; subdue inner excitement

CURVE: This helps to create beauty; make something beautiful. This is good to enhance creativity.

DIVINE: This one will help you work miracles or accomplish extraordinary things, it increases personal ability.

DOWN: This helps you become more humble. People don't like braggarts , this will help eliminate that trait in you if bragging is a problem for you.

FOREVER: This will help you keep a secret .

HELP: This helps eliminate indecision or uncertainty and increases focus.

HOLD: This helps to build character.

Now I will briefly go into Switchword combinations or "Switchphrases". Some teachers suggest that before moving on to Switchphrases, you should master the individual Switchwords. Personally, I did not find this necessary. I used Switchphrases immediately with great results. Whether you want to use the words individually or in a phrase will ultimately be your decision. Whatever feels right to you. I use them both.

I use the SwitchPhrase UP-MOVE-HALFWAY during my runs and I find this Switchphrase works for me better than using them individually, especially while running.

The purpose of switchphrases is to enhance the power of an individual request. I personally do not think the order of the words is very important when creating a switchphrase, but some do. If it works, that's all that matters in the end.

Here is an Example: Let's say you want to attract a substantial financial gain, you can use the following Switchphrase:

FIND-DIVINE-COUNT-TOGETHER

Notice in the above Switchphrase we have both Switchwords for money "Find" and "Count". We have "Divine" in order to align the request with Divine intentions and the Switchword "Together" is used as the master switchword to make it all come together. So In essence the phrase means " May my desire for abundance and divine will come together to make it so." The subconscious mind has no time to interpret the switchwords, it simply switches the energy on. If you were to say the meaning instead " May my desire for abundance and divine will come together to make it so." The subconscious mind will kick that out immediately since it runs counter to your current experience of lack.

Here are a few more examples of Switchphrases you can use for various situations.
To defeat self limiting beliefs about money use LOVE-COUNT or COUNT-LOVE.
To gain a sense of clarity use CRYSTAL-QUIET.
To finish a long laborious process use HALFWAY-DONE.
To solve a dilemma or problem you are having you can use DIVINE-HELP. Or CRYSTAL-HELP.

Enjoy writing more use GIGGLE-ACT.
To feel physically vibrant you can use DIVINE-CHANGE OR DIVINE-CHANGE-TOGETHER.

To improve your studying before an exam you can use DIVINE-CARE or CARE-TOGETHER.
To let go of an addiction POSTPONE-SAVE, use this especially for alcoholism.
To make a huge transformation in your life with great ability you can use DIVINE-ACT.
These are of course just a few. Please remember there really isn't any way to get this wrong. String as many words as you feel comfortable with and that is practical for you. You don't want the Switchphrases to be so long that you won't remember the combination. However, there aren't hard and fast rules to this. Please feel free to make any combination you desire and with as many as you like. You can also repeat a Switchword within a switchphrase more than once as well.

Alright, we are just a paragraph or two away from Part 2 where you will find the exercises. Let me now show you how you can create your own Switchwords that resonate with you personally.

The process of discovering personal Switchwords is quite easy:

Sit comfortably where you will not be disturbed for 5 or 10 minutes. Think about what it is you want a Switchword for. When you have the intention in mind say "Together, Together, Together, Together, Together, Together, Together, Together, " That's 8 times and listen to the first word that comes into your mind. Don't worry if the word sounds silly, that's your subconscious mind giving you a personal Switchword. You don't need to share it with anyone. Once you have your own switchword you can use it like any other switchword and in combination with others. I did this process when I wanted motivation for tasks and the word "Tiger" came out. Every time I say Tiger, I feel a surge of motivation. The Switchwords that are created by other people are known as " Broad Switchwords".. Ok, that's it, now we are on to part 2. I know I supplied you with a ton of information, but it was necessary. Knowledge is potential power, let's use this knowledge now to potentiate the power in you.

The Switchwords in this chapter have been gleaned from the following sources: James T. Mangan The Secret of Perfect Living. Shunyam Nirav Switchwords " Easily Give to You Whatever You Want in Life" and Kat Millers Wonderful site http://.www.blueiris.org

CHAPTER 7: PUTTING THE PIECES TOGETHER

You made it!

We are now going to put all the pieces together. I will pick 5 major life themes that many, if not all people struggle with at one point in their lives. Each theme will have 3 rounds of tapping.

Round 1. Is the acknowledgement sequence. This round will send a message to your mind that you acknowledge the issue at hand.
Round 2. Is the desired outcome sequence. This will send a message to the mind that a preferred desired outcome is desired.
Round 3. Is the switchword sequence. In this sequences we tap the meridian points stating the switchword we have chosen.

I will cover the following themes:
• General Health.
• Financial life.
• General Fitness.
• Relationships.
• Spiritual growth.

I will pick one issue in each theme and illustrate how to go through the exercises. You can, of course, use this for all issues you may have, not just the ones I am illustrating here.

Basic instructions before you start any session:
Find a place where you will not be disturbed. This shouldn't take more than 3 or 4 minutes tops. You can, however, choose to make this as long as you like.

1. Have the image with the Meridian points handy so you will know which areas to tap when we go through the rounds. I will also state which points to tap.
2. Select the Switchword or switchphrases that apply to your particular issue.
3. Do the issue acknowledgement sequence.
4. Do the desired outcome sequence.
5. Do the switchword sequence.

A quick tip: I find that after you do the acknowledgment sequence and desired outcome sequence you do not have to revisit them again. After you do all 3 sequences you can simply say the chosen switchword or switchphrases throughout the day and that's all it will take to keep the wheels of change moving. Say them as often as you like. If you do feel that you need to do the acknowledgment sequence and desired outcome sequences again you may do so without worry.
And that's it really. Pretty simple. Let's start a few sessions.

General Health
In this example we will choose Chronic pain as the health issue we want to address.

Assuming you either have the image of the meridian points handy or you have memorized them, we will now select the appropriate switchword. In this case we will select the switchword CHANGE you can also use the switchword BE. You can use them together if you like. For this example I will use CHANGE.

Acknowledgement sequence: Please repeat out loud or to yourself the following words as you tap the meridian points. (You can use your choice of words as well, this is just an example)

Karate Chop Point: Although I have this chronic pain, I am open and willing to love myself anyway.
Eye Brow Point: I feel this pain in my body.
Side of Eye Point: I feel this pain in my body and I do not know what it means.
Under Eye Point: I feel this pain in my body.
Under Nose Point: I feel this pain in my body, I can't deny it any longer.
Chin Point: I realize I have pain and I am willing to understand it.
Collar Bone Point: I feel this pain and I know it is trying to tell me something. But what?
Under Arm point: This pain has overstayed its welcome.
Top of head point: This pain in my body.
(Take a deep breath, this concludes the acknowledgment sequence.)

Desired outcome sequence: Please repeat out loud or to yourself the following words as you tap the meridian points. (You can use your choice of words as well, this is just an example)

Karate Chop Point: Although I have this chronic pain, I am open and willing to love myself anyway.

Eye Brow Point: I feel this pain in my body and I am willing to let it go TODAY.

Side of Eye Point: This pain has no room in my life anymore.

Under Eye Point: I am willing to do what it takes to get rid of this pain.

Under Nose Point: I choose to live a pain free life from now on.

Chin Point: I realize this pain will go away.

Collar Bone Point: I release this pain once and for all.

Under Arm point: This pain has overstayed its welcome.

Top of head point: This pain in my body will be gone and will never return.

(Take a deep breath, this concludes the desired outcome sequence.)

The Switchword sequence: Please repeat out loud or to yourself the following Switchword/s as you tap the meridian points. You can say the switchwords words as many times as you want at every Meridian point. I say them 5 times in my own practice and will use that as the example. (You can use Switchphrases as well)

Karate Chop Point: CHANGE, CHANGE, CHANGE, CHANGE, CHANGE

Eye Brow Point: CHANGE, CHANGE, CHANGE, CHANGE, CHANGE

Side of Eye Point: CHANGE, CHANGE, CHANGE, CHANGE, CHANGE

Under Eye Point: CHANGE, CHANGE, CHANGE, CHANGE, CHANGE

Under Nose Point: CHANGE, CHANGE, CHANGE, CHANGE, CHANGE
Chin Point: CHANGE, CHANGE, CHANGE, CHANGE, CHANGE
Collar Bone Point: CHANGE, CHANGE, CHANGE, CHANGE, CHANGE
Under Arm point: CHANGE, CHANGE, CHANGE, CHANGE, CHANGE
Top of head point: CHANGE, CHANGE, CHANGE, CHANGE, CHANGE
END OF SEQUENCE.

That's it, pretty simple right? You just started a cascade of change throughout your mind and I bet you will feel the shift either right away or in a very short period of time. You may notice the pain has disappeared completely or it started to move. In some rare cases the pain got worse for a moment, that is okay, keep at it. The subconscious mind was rattled. This is a good thing...Change is on its way.

Financial Life

In this example we will chose excessive debt as the financial issue we want to address.

Assuming you either have the image of the meridian points handy or you have memorized them, we will now select the appropriate switchword. In this case we will select the switchword CANCEL you can also use the switchwords COUNT or FIND. You can use them together if you like. For this example I will use CANCEL.

Acknowledgement sequence: Please repeat out loud or to yourself the following words as you tap the meridian points. (You can use your choice of words as well, this is just an example)

Karate Chop Point: Although I have this crushing debt, I am open and willing to love myself anyway.

Eye Brow Point: I feel this debt overwhelm me and I really don't like it.

Side of Eye Point: The debt keeps piling up.

Under Eye Point: I am having a very hard time making ends meet because of my debt.

Under Nose Point: I can't deny this debt any longer.

Chin Point: I realize I have debt and I am willing to understand it.

Collar Bone Point: This debt is stopping me from living a full life.

Under Arm point: The pain of this debt is nagging me.

Top of head point: This crushing debt that I have

(Take a deep breath, this concludes the acknowledgment sequence.)

Desired outcome sequence: Please repeat out loud or to yourself the following words as you tap the meridian points. (You can use your choice of words as well, this is just an example)

Karate Chop Point: Although I have this crushing debt, I am open and willing to love myself anyway.
Eye Brow Point: I see this debt in front of me and I am willing to get rid of it.
Side of Eye Point: This debt has no room in my life anymore.
Under Eye Point: I am willing to do what it takes to get rid of this debt.
Under Nose Point: I choose to live debt free life from now on.
Chin Point: I realize this debt will be resolved.
Collar Bone Point: I release this debt once and for all.
Under Arm point: This debt has overstayed its welcome.
Top of head point: I intend to be debt free for the rest of my life.
(Take a deep breath, this concludes the desired outcome sequence.)

The Switchword sequence: Please repeat out loud or to yourself the following Switchword/s as you tap the meridian points. You can say the switchwords words as many times as you want at every Meridian point. I say them 5 times in my own practice and will use that as the example. (You can use Switchphrases as well)

Karate Chop Point:
CANCEL,CANCEL,CANCEL,CANCEL,CANCEL
Eye Brow Point:
CANCEL,CANCEL,CANCEL,CANCEL,CANCEL
Side of Eye Point:
CANCEL,CANCEL,CANCEL,CANCEL,CANCEL
Under Eye Point:
CANCEL,CANCEL,CANCEL,CANCEL,CANCEL
Under Nose Point:
CANCEL,CANCEL,CANCEL,CANCEL,CANCEL
Chin Point: CANCEL,CANCEL,CANCEL,CANCEL,CANCEL
Collar Bone Point:
CANCEL,CANCEL,CANCEL,CANCEL,CANCEL
Under Arm point:
CANCEL,CANCEL,CANCEL,CANCEL,CANCEL
Top of head point:
CANCEL,CANCEL,CANCEL,CANCEL,CANCEL
END OF SEQUENCE.

This particular sequence is very strong. I did this with 2 people I know and as they did the switchword sequences they felt this motivation to get themselves out of debt once and for all. The surge of energy they received was amazing. If you are in debt and want to get rid of it, I suggest this sequence highly.

General Fitness

In this example we will choose overeating as the general fitness issue we want to address.

Assuming you either have the image of the meridian points

handy or you have memorized them, we will now select the appropriate switchword. In this case we will select the switchword CUT you can also use the switchwords POSTSPONE or SAVE. You can use them together if you like. For this example I will use CUT.

Acknowledgement sequence: Please repeat out loud or to yourself the following words as you tap the meridian points. (You can use your choice of words as well, this is just an example)

Karate Chop Point: Although I have this problem with overeating, I am open and willing to love myself anyway.
Eye Brow Point: I overeat and I really want to stop.
Side of Eye Point: My overeating is causing me to gain weight.
Under Eye Point: I am having a very hard time with overeating.
Under Nose Point: I cant deny this overeating problem that I have any longer.
Chin Point: I realize I overeat, but don't know why.
Collar Bone Point: Overeating is destroying myself esteem.
Under Arm point: Overeating causes me a lot of pain.
Top of head point: My overeating.
(Take a deep breath, this concludes the acknowledgment sequence.)

Desired outcome sequence: Please repeat out loud or to yourself the following words as you tap the meridian points. (You can use your choice of words as well, this is just an example)

Karate Chop Point: Although I have this problem with overeating, I am open and willing to love myself anyway.
Eye Brow Point: I am willing to conquer this overeating issue i have once and for all.
Side of Eye Point: I am willing to let go of this overeating issue I have.
Under Eye Point: I am willing to do what it takes to stop overeating.
Under Nose Point: I choose to eat sensibly.
Chin Point: I realize this overeating issue can be resolved.
Collar Bone Point: I choose to release my need to overeat.
Under Arm point: Overeating has overstayed its welcome.
Top of head point: I intend to eat sensibly for the rest of my life.
(Take a deep breath, this concludes the desired outcome sequence.)

The Switchword sequence: Please repeat out loud or to yourself the following Switchword/s as you tap the meridian points. You can say the switchwords words as many times as you want at every Meridian point. I say them 5 times in my own practice and will use that as the example. (You can use Switchphrases as well)

Karate Chop Point: CUT, CUT,CUT,CUT,CUT
Eye Brow Point: CUT, CUT,CUT,CUT,CUT
Side of Eye Point: CUT, CUT,CUT,CUT,CUT
Under Eye Point: CUT, CUT,CUT,CUT,CUT
Under Nose Point: CUT, CUT,CUT,CUT,CUT
Chin Point: CUT, CUT,CUT,CUT,CUT

Collar Bone Point: CUT, CUT,CUT,CUT,CUT
Under Arm point: CUT, CUT,CUT,CUT,CUT
Top of head point: CUT, CUT,CUT,CUT,CUT
150
END OF SEQUENCE.

Overeating is a huge problem and is the number one cause of the obesity epidemic several countries are facing. Barring organic or hormonal dysfunction, overeating is mainly a habit and not a sickness. For those who overeat out of habit, I recommend this sequence above. I also recommend it for those who have hormonal imbalances because I have witnessed on several occasions that this sequence helps clear the mind and in that clear state solution can be found. Solutions that may help you control overeating and its effects.

Relationships

In this example we will choose the fear of intimacy as the related issue we want to address.

Assuming you either have the image of the meridian points handy or you have memorized them, we will now select the appropriate switchword. In this case we will select the switchword OPEN you can also use the switchwords BE or HOLE. You can use them together if you like. For this example I will use OPEN.

Acknowledgement sequence: Please repeat out loud or to yourself the following words as you tap the meridian points. (You can use your choice of words as well, this is just an example)

Karate Chop Point: Although I feel closed off to love, I am open and willing to love myself anyway.
Eye Brow Point: I am afraid to love again and I really want to stop being this way.
Side of Eye Point: My fear of getting hurt is denying me so much in my life.
Under Eye Point: I am having a very hard time letting people in.
Under Nose Point: I can't deny my fear of intimacy any longer.
Chin Point: I realize how this fear of intimacy is ruining my life.
Collar Bone Point: My fear of intimacy and relationships is destroying my self esteem.
Under Arm point: The Fear of intimacy that I have infects all aspects of my life .
Top of head point: My fear of intimacy.
(Take a deep breath, this concludes the acknowledgment sequence.)

Desired outcome sequence: Please repeat out loud or to yourself the following words as you tap the meridian points. (You can use your choice of words as well, this is just an example)

Karate Chop Point: Although I feel closed off to love, I am open and willing to love myself anyway.
Eye Brow Point: I am willing to conquer this fear of intimacy issue I have once and for all.
Side of Eye Point: I am willing to let go of this fear of intimacy and start living .

Under Eye Point: I am willing to do what it takes to reduce my fear of intimacy.
Under Nose Point: I intend to love again.
Chin Point: I realize this fear of intimacy can be resolved.
Collar Bone Point: I choose to release any anxiety I have about relationships.
Under Arm point: This loneliness has overstayed its welcome.
Top of head point: I intend to embrace love and intimacy with courage.
(Take a deep breath, this concludes the desired outcome sequence.)

The Switchword sequence: Please repeat out loud or to yourself the following Switchword/s as you tap the meridian points. You can say the switchwords words as many times as you want at every Meridian point. I say them 5 times in my own practice and will use that as the example. (You can use Switchphrases as well)

Karate Chop Point: OPEN, OPEN, OPEN, OPEN, OPEN
Eye Brow Point: OPEN, OPEN, OPEN, OPEN, OPEN
Side of Eye Point: OPEN, OPEN, OPEN, OPEN, OPEN
Under Eye Point: OPEN, OPEN, OPEN, OPEN, OPEN
Under Nose Point: OPEN, OPEN, OPEN, OPEN, OPEN
Chin Point: OPEN, OPEN, OPEN, OPEN, OPEN
Collar Bone Point: OPEN, OPEN, OPEN, OPEN, OPEN
Under Arm point: OPEN, OPEN, OPEN, OPEN, OPEN
Top of head point: OPEN, OPEN, OPEN, OPEN, OPEN
END OF SEQUENCE.

This sequence is a tough one for many people. I know it was for me. As I stated earlier in the book one of my main issues was allowing myself to be in a relationship after being hurt a few times. My defense mechanisms were quite strong. When I did the acknowledgement sequences I thought I was going to have a panic attack. I got so anxious. This of course is a sign that the issue needed to be addressed. Don't be surprised if you get a little anxiety from some of these sequences, it simply a sign that you are finally addressing the issue and working on its resolution. Stick with it.

Spiritual growth.

In this example we will choose a deeper connection to the divine/universe as the spiritual issue we want to address. Assuming you either have the image of the meridian points handy or you have memorized them, we will now select the appropriate switchword. In this case I will use two. we will select the switchphrase DIVINE-TOGETHER. These two work very well for deepening your spiritual connection to God/Divine/Universe.

Acknowledgement sequence: Please repeat out loud or to yourself the following words as you tap the meridian points. (You can use your choice of words as well, this is just an example)

Karate Chop Point: Although I feel cut off from my divine source, I intend to stay loving and connected with myself anyway.
Eye Brow Point: This feeling of not being connected to God/universe causes me great pain.
Side of Eye Point: I feel like I am spiritually empty.

Under Eye Point: I am having a very hard time feeling that spiritual connection.
Under Nose Point: I can't deny this feeling of detachment with the divine anymore.
Chin Point: I realize this lack of spiritual connection makes my life feel hollow.
Collar Bone Point: My feeling that I am not connected to source makes me feel afraid and alone.
Under Arm point: This spiritual void in my life makes me feel depressed.
Top of head point: My lack of connection with source energy.
(Take a deep breath, this concludes the acknowledgment sequence.)

Desired outcome sequence: Please repeat out loud or to yourself the following words as you tap the meridian points. (You can use your choice of words as well, this is just an example)

Karate Chop Point: Although I feel cut off from my divine source, I intend to stay loving and connected with myself anyway.
Eye Brow Point: I know I am part of the divine and thus my feeling of separation is an illusion.
Side of Eye Point: I am willing to let go and let God .
Under Eye Point: I am willing to create a daily mindfulness practice to reconnect.
Under Nose Point: I intend to cultivate my spirituality.
Chin Point: I realize this feeling of disconnection is an illusion and I am willing to see it that way.
Collar Bone Point: I realize God loves all, including me.
Under Arm point: Spirituality is my lifeblood.
Top of head point: I intend to see spirit in everything that I do.

(Take a deep breath, this concludes the desired outcome sequence.)

The Switchword sequence: Please repeat out loud or to yourself the following Switchword/s as you tap the meridian points. You can say the switchwords words as many times as you want at every Meridian point. I say them 5 times in my own practice and will use that as the example. (You can use Switchphrases as well)

Karate Chop Point: DIVINE-TOGETHER, DIVINE-TOGETHER, DIVINE-TOGETHER, DIVINE-TOGETHER, DIVINE-TOGETHER.
Eye Brow Point: DIVINE-TOGETHER, DIVINE-TOGETHER, DIVINE-TOGETHER, DIVINE-TOGETHER, DIVINE-TOGETHER.
Side of Eye Point: DIVINE-TOGETHER, DIVINE-TOGETHER, DIVINE-TOGETHER, DIVINE-TOGETHER, DIVINE-TOGETHER.
Under Eye Point: DIVINE-TOGETHER, DIVINE-TOGETHER, DIVINE-TOGETHER, DIVINE-TOGETHER, DIVINE-TOGETHER.
Under Nose Point: DIVINE-TOGETHER, DIVINE-TOGETHER, DIVINE-TOGETHER, DIVINE-TOGETHER, DIVINE-TOGETHER.
Chin Point: DIVINE-TOGETHER, DIVINE-TOGETHER, DIVINE-TOGETHER, DIVINE-TOGETHER, DIVINE-TOGETHER.
Collar Bone Point: DIVINE-TOGETHER, DIVINE-TOGETHER, DIVINE-TOGETHER, DIVINE-TOGETHER, DIVINE-TOGETHER.
Under Arm point: DIVINE-TOGETHER, DIVINE-

TOGETHER, DIVINE-TOGETHER, DIVINE-TOGETHER, DIVINE-TOGETHER.
Top of head point: DIVINE-TOGETHER, DIVINE-TOGETHER, DIVINE-TOGETHER, DIVINE-TOGETHER, DIVINE-TOGETHER.
END OF SEQUENCE.

I love this sequence, it is very powerful. I am sure that once you do this sequence once, you will have goosebumps. The divine is ever present and your subconscious mind is a perfect receiver of divine energy. Now all you need to do is make it work positively in your life and the above exercises will help you do that.

There you have it, the above exercises are all you need to learn in order to get Switchwords to work for you. Please feel free to adapt this to your own liking. As you can see this is very easy and I hope it will bring you the change that you so very much need in your life.

CONCLUSION

We have come to the end of our time here and I want to thank you from the bottom of my heart for allowing me to spend this time with you. I know I provided you with a lot of information. I know some of you may even think the whole idea of switchwords is silly, but in the end, if it works for you, that's all that matters.

It took me several years to get to the point where I found something that worked well and regularly. This book is the culmination of that quest. This book could have been several hundred pages longer but for our purposes I wanted to provide clear cut transformational material. This was not a book of profound spiritual truths and sayings but rather, a practical guide.

I hope this book will help you in all your endeavors.

To find out more about other SWITCHWORD Related Products that can take your switchword Practice to a new level please visit:

http://www.Switchwordmiracles.com

Thank you again for sharing your time with me.

Contact Information

Doron Alon is the author of 10 books, owner of the publishing company Numinosity Press Inc.

For the last four years, Doron has dedicated every waking moment to designing Spiritual Techniques that help people break through their limitations to achieve success and inner peace in their lives. This focus has culminated in the creation of Switchword Subliminals: The ultimate subliminal audio/video programs and the Best Seller , Switchword Miracles .

Doron's background and 23 years of experience in meditation training, Meridian tapping (also known as E.F.T), Subliminal Messaging, Law of Attraction and more has helped him to focus on the techniques that provide the best results, and collate them for you in an easy to understand format. He is also a history buff and will be releasing books in that genre as well.

Want to know more? Then scroll down the page and check out the different eBooks Doron has published.

Please feel free to email me at doron@switchwordmiracles.com

For Other Books By Doron please visit his author page at

http://www.amazon.com/author/doronalon

15470906R00065

Printed in Great Britain
by Amazon